The
JOURNEY WITHIN

The
JOURNEY
WITHIN

7 Phases of Transformation for Self-Realization

ARDA OZDEMIR

Author of *Emotional Mastery for Relationships*

RISE 2 REALIZE

Copyright © 2025 Arda Ozdemir

All rights reserved.

No part of this book may be reproduced, or stored in a retrieval system, or transmitted in any form or by any means, electronic, mechanical, photocopying, recording, or otherwise, without express written permission of the publisher.

The Journey Within is for informational and educational purposes only. The information contained in this guidebook is based on the author's own experience and not intended to diagnose, prescribe, treat, or cure any disease or mental condition, or to replace the services of a licensed therapist, mental health care provider, or physician.

Published by Rise 2 Realize LLC, Los Altos, CA www.rise2realize.com

Developmental and Copyediting: Lore Alexander www.scribeandsunshine.com
Content Advisor: Elizabeth Ouellette www.bestlifeevercoaching.org
Cover Design: Kathryn Campbell www.inkbooksdesign.com
Image Credit: Tomas Hensrud Gulla / Midjourney
Author photo: Tati Scutelnic www.tatiratita.com

ISBN (paperback): 978-0-9898104-4-9

First edition

Printed in the United States of America

RISE 2 REALIZE

The only difference between the saint and the sinner is that every saint has a past, and every sinner has a future.

—Oscar Wilde

CONTENTS

Introduction	Discovering a New Life	1
Phase 1	Becoming Self-Aware	9
Phase 2	Understanding Your Conditioned Self	31
Phase 3	Expanding Your Boundaries	51
Phase 4	Bringing Peace to Your Inner Conflict	67
Phase 5	Discovering What's Important to You	79
Phase 6	Coming Out of Your Shell	103
Phase 7	Living with Purpose	117
Conclusion	Building Trust and Flow	131
	About the Author	139

INTRODUCTION

Discovering a New Life

I want my money back! I was fooled! Growing up, everybody told me to chase happiness. I did. They told me to acquire it from all the resources outside myself. I did. They told me to work hard and marry wise. I did. But nothing had prepared me for what I was about to experience, a complete rupture of identity, about six months before my fortieth birthday.

It was July 2006. It had been almost two years since I started suffering from chronic sinus infections and regular occurrences of bronchitis and pneumonia. As if I was on a preset schedule, every other month, I would get sick and spend my weekends locked in my house dealing with a stuffy nose and constant coughing. During those times, my postnasal drip would irritate my lungs so bad that I would hardly get any sleep most nights.

To put it mildly, in those years, my life simply sucked. It was horrible. I didn't have energy for anything else other than getting up in the morning to go to work, then coming home late, having some dinner, and watching TV until I forgot everything, then falling asleep to repeat the same miserable cycle again the next morning.

However, if you met me on the street or at a bar, you would have thought I had a wonderful life. And you'd have been correct from the outside. I was at the top of my career, holding a VP of finance position at a high-tech start-up in Silicon Valley, California. I had been happily married for fifteen years to my best friend with whom

I traveled the world and lived in Istanbul, Sydney, and San Francisco. We lived in a beautiful home on Telegraph Hill, drove nice cars, and spent our vacations in Europe.

I thought I had everything. I was happy. But then, what was wrong with my body? Why was it breaking down?

I've always believed in a close connection between the mind and the body. When I was asking these questions and wondering how I got here, a deep urge was rising within me to investigate the heck out of my life and deeply understand the underlying reasons for my deteriorating health despite my outwardly happy life.

Right around that time, my wife, who was concerned about my physical state and inability to live a quality life, slipped a note with a name and phone number for an intuitive healer in New York. Her name was Naz McSweeney. Even though I was skeptical in the beginning, I decided to give it a shot. I remember that call like it was yesterday. I was in my living room in San Francisco, and she was on the phone telling me all about my Self.

I said I wanted to investigate how I got to this point in my life, but I didn't expect the answers to be revealed to me so bluntly and so clearly. I felt like I'd been thrown under an ice-cold shower while I was expecting a warm, soothing bath. She saw all my childhood traumas, all my insecurities, all my shortcomings. She told me about my wrong turns and bad decisions and why I had done the things the way I did. She reflected on my life and told me with her softest and most caring voice that the life I was born to live was supposed to be completely different from the current one—the one I had built with sweat and blood over the last four decades.

I'd like to claim innocence here! Since the day I set foot onto the grounds of my elementary school, I naively followed every command my parents and my teachers gave me. I obeyed the rules of society. I met everyone's expectations without teetering. But now, I was hearing for the first time in my life that everything I'd done was for the wrong reasons. Apparently, it was all for safety and security. What?!?! How was I supposed to know that?

Hearing all of that, all at once, affected me deeply. I experienced a big shock to my center, to my identity, that I'd never felt before. It was like a punch in my stomach that lingered and grew exponentially into a nauseating pit in my core. Everything started crumbling down like a house of cards. I had to get out of the house. I immediately walked out of the door and started walking.

After a good half hour, I found myself in Washington Square Park, a nearby park in North Beach, the Italian neighborhood of San Francisco, which is known for its great restaurants, cheerful cafés, vibrant bars, and beautiful streets full of people. I sat down in complete exhaustion, catching my breath from hyperventilation.

My eyes slowly looked up and gazed around. There were a lot of people hanging out in the park, in probably one of the liveliest corners of the city. They all seemed to be so happy. They threw frisbees to each other. They laughed out loud at each other's jokes. They shared food and drank wine as they enjoyed their picnics together. Couples embraced each other on warm blankets.

I thought I would have felt jealous of them or envious of their happiness. Yet all of that meant nothing to me. Maybe it was the growing emptiness I started to sense in my chest that made me numb against these happy faces. I feared that I was no longer part of them. I was rapidly losing my ground. I was scared that the life I'd created—my marriage, my career, the place I held in society, the character I'd developed—was going to falter. I felt deeply depressed.

I will never forget that day, that hour! It was one of the darkest moments of my life. Later on, I learned what I was going through right there and then was called "death before dying" in Sufi spiritual teachings. I didn't know that most people experience such profound disconnection from everything when they are forced to question their life and their ego.

Such deep inquiry takes the person through the darkest night of the soul and leads them to a profound awakening to the transformation of their life. Yes, it was very painful. Yes, it was a big, giant hole I felt in the middle of my body. Yes, that emptiness took away my safety harnesses, guard rails, and all the branches I'd been grasping onto and left me naked, vulnerable, and plummeting in midair.

Yet I decided to open my eyes to what was hidden within me. I couldn't stand the pain of fakeness anymore and felt I had to do something about it. The moment I put such a strong intention in my mind, I started walking the glorious path of personal awakening and transformation, where everything in my life changed dramatically from that day onward.

What you are about to read in this book are the strategies and techniques that helped me wake up to my true nature and live a life beyond my dreams. From sitting on that bench, completely collapsed mentally, physically, and emotionally, and absolutely disconnected from everything, all the way to today, where I regularly flow with life, experiencing joy, ease, and deep meaning. Over the years, through this amazing high flow, I've been able to identify my personal values that are aligned with my core essence, which ultimately guided me to my place in the world as a spiritual mentor to those who are ready to awaken.

Such a transformation journey doesn't necessarily mean that you will experience death before dying as severely as I did or eventually quit your job to become a coach and dedicate your life to helping others as I did. No, your experience will be completely different and perfectly unique to you.

However, you will discover your calling, whatever that may be. Whether it's having the most deeply loving relationship, or pursuing the most fulfilling career, or becoming the best parent you can be, at the end of this journey, you'll realize the special purpose of your life and find your meaningful place in this world.

Connecting with that special calling is what the Journey Within offers. By following specific steps, you'll eventually reach a deep understanding of your character, in a sense, who you are and why you built your life the way you did.

During this awakening process, you'll also gain profound insights into your behaviors, actions, and preprogrammed automatic reactions and see why you do things the way you do. This invaluable self-knowledge about your ego structure and psyche will eventually help you break free from your old, established, negative, and limiting patterns and bring you the opportunity to be the best and most real version of yourself.

What you do with the self-awareness you gain during your Journey Within is completely up to you. However, if you choose to walk the path of personal transformation toward self-realization, you'll eventually get to know your true essence and experience joy, fulfillment, and purpose as you naturally embrace life and taste its magic.

Like a mad scientist, I took copious notes about every step I took during my Journey Within over the last fifteen years and analyzed them and synthesized them to come up with seven distinct phases of transformation that everybody seems to go through from a stagnant, unfulfilling life to one where they experience a life with meaning and purpose.

In this book, I present these phases in great detail with specific techniques and strategies so that you can also go through a similar life-changing journey, where you'll encounter deep insights and discover profound answers to your existential questions and eventually encounter what's within you—your Real Self. Each phase offers experiments for you to try in your own life; in a sense, you'll become the mad scientist yourself and will draw your own conclusions from the results you experience. With this knowledge, you can change the trajectory of your life for the better.

What's waiting for you ahead is to inevitably confirm to yourself what you already know: that there's more to life than mediocrity and dissatisfaction, which is inherently built in to a life where all decisions are made by the underlying fears to hedge the uncertainty of life with safety and security.

Once you step on this path, you'll gradually become less reliant on the ways you used to validate yourself. The inauthentic external goals that society has pressured you to follow will slowly lose their glamour and no longer offer satisfaction. In a sense, you'll no longer be bound by society's norms, expectations from your parents, or the dogma of your community. Instead, you'll learn to live only by your own values, which are real, true, and meaningful to you.

You may feel that following your own values may alienate you from your family, from your career, or from your community. Even though you experience big shifts in your personal and professional life, it doesn't necessarily mean you have to leave your relationship, your job, your friends, your community, or the positions you currently hold.

On the contrary, you'll seize opportunities to improve your relationships, deepen your role in your family, bring more meaning to your job, become a more consciously aware parent, form deeper connections with your friends, or receive more recognition and respect in your community. The more you sincerely stay connected to your personal and spiritual goals, and take conscious efforts in your Journey Within, the more closely aligned your life will be with your true nature and with everyone around you.

When you feel this grand shift, your calling slowly emerges right in front of your eyes. The purpose of your life becomes clearer. Your unique place in the world appears. Without any agenda, you authentically express your Real Self. Through this genuine self-expression, you feel guided step by step down the path to self-realization without feeling bound, restricted, or limited by any external goals, expectations, or obligations.

The level of diligence, commitment, and consistency you show on this journey determines how successful you are going to be in becoming your Real Self. Of course, you will not be alone on this journey. The seven phases of personal transformation offer specific strategies and techniques and provide weekly assignments that are laid out for you in each phase to help you reach your destination. You can also register for free for my seven-week Journey Within workshop at www.R2R.org/journey-within.

Ultimately, this is your reference book that you can keep coming back to with your deep introspections, profound insights, and unique experiences. The goal of such a resourceful book, in a way a guidebook, is to be the light that shines on each and every step you take, as you're the only one who can walk this path with its pain and its glory.

Whether you can complete such an arduous journey is up to you. However, one thing is certain: when you follow the steps of the Journey Within, you have no choice but to become your Real Self.

PHASE 1

BECOMING SELF-AWARE

When you know your current coordinates, it's easier to reach the destination you desire. For that reason, it's no surprise that your Journey Within starts with becoming aware of who you are today. As we discussed earlier, the reason your current life is not as fulfilling as it should be is because the way you show up today is not "real." This first phase of your transformation journey is an invitation to find out who that "Not-Real" Self is. After all, you feel unfulfilled because you don't live as the best version of yourself. You rarely present your true essence. However, things are about to change around here.

You may wonder, who is this Not-Real Self? Who is this person that lives a certain life: has a spouse or is single, or is a parent or has no kids, or works at a job or struggles to keep one, or goes on errands or lazes around all day, or gets promotions or constantly complains about being stuck at their forever position, or goes on dates or never gets a date, or meets with friends or feels lonely in their apartment, or frequently visits their parents or never sees or talks to them.

Who are you really?

Who or what kind of personalities do you play in all these interactions? What kind of identity do you carry in life? What is your specific role in your relationships? Who is your persona you act out with others?

Did you know the Latin root of the word *persona* means "mask" or "character" played by an actor? During such play, the character fits into the scripted drama, and the actor can't manipulate their accepted role or character. They stay true to their part and act accordingly. By wearing such a mask, an actor only reflects what's on the surface, hiding the "real" person underneath.

What are these masks we wear? Why do we carry them so religiously as if our lives depend on the strength of such disguises? After working with more than six thousand clients in the last fifteen years, I've been shocked to discover that none of us are real. When we put all personas together, two distinct categories emerge that we constantly display in our daily interactions.

I call the first one the Vulnerable Self. This persona contains our insecurities that resulted from early traumatic and emotionally painful experiences that we had in our past.

The second one is called the Conditioned Self. This persona, on the other hand, is the one who tries to hide the insecurities of our Vulnerable Self to prevent the outside world from noticing them.

In a sense, the Conditioned Self is the protector of the Vulnerable Self, like a big brother. He does the job by wearing a thick mask. He uses this mask very strategically, pretending to be this or that so no one sees his little brother, the Vulnerable Self, as weak and insecure.

Of course, these two personas clash all the time. They create a never-ending internal conflict loop, like how two siblings behave with each other. They carry opposing goals within you. Their goal is to pull you in the directions of their liking, the way they want you to think, feel, and behave. As a result, you get caught in the middle. You get lost in this tug-of-war between brothers. Due to their confusing and conflicting agendas, they eventually become the source of your mental and emotional suffering.

You're not the only one who experiences this. Everyone is subject to this internal conflict and exposed to such suffering. Hence, where you are today is not necessarily where you have to be in the future. Once you decipher the puzzle of these opposing personas, you can get out of the debilitating dilemma between the two. That's when you create a better life for yourself. Through becoming aware of these characters, you slowly break free from the safe and secure yet monotonous life they've built for you. The personal freedom you gain from this expanded self-awareness eventually leads you to your profound self-realization.

ORIGINS OF THE VULNERABLE SELF

Shall we start with the first persona? How does the Vulnerable Self come into being?

Growing up, we're all exposed to a variety of traumatic and hurtful experiences. Much of the time, the emotional wound these events cause is not immediately obvious to us. If it's a severely intense physical and emotional trauma or abuse, we tend to completely suppress the painful feelings that we experience in that moment. If it's a psychological trauma, we tend to omit its emotional pain and go on with our lives without knowing how deeply it affected our personality.

For example, when parents ask their kid why they haven't performed better in school, even though they have almost all A's on their scorecard, except for two B's, the child feels inadequate, unrecognized, devalued, and like a failure. What happens to those feelings? They become the child's insecurity that they still carry in their adult life.

Examples where the trauma is not obvious are plenty.

When parents are never around and always leave one kid's care to an older sibling or sometimes to grandparents, the kid feels abandoned, lonely, and unimportant.

When parents criticize their kids and mock them whenever they do something wrong, the kids feel incompetent, put down, and dismissed.

When parents experience financial difficulty and emphasize how important it is to save every penny for the future, the kid feels financially insecure, mistrust, and anxiety well into their adult life, even though they may have plenty of money in the bank.

When parents get divorced and can't agree on a visitation schedule, the kid may end up spending most of their time with one parent and feel abandoned, betrayed, and worthless.

You may have experienced some of these and maybe many more situations where you had no idea how they affected you mentally and emotionally because they are all still tucked away into the depths of your subconscious. As long as these emotional wounds remain unprocessed, what happened in the past will keep happening to you today. During your Journey Within, you'll learn how to process them so you can break free from your subconscious programming and step out of the bounds of the past that make your current life unfulfilling.

How can you process your emotional wounds that are buried in your subconscious? By identifying them during your drama cycles.

Conflicts where others elicit emotional reactions in you carry so much information about your subconscious programming and the intimate details about your Vulnerable Self. Unfortunately, you miss acquiring such valuable self-knowledge due to the intensity of your emotional reactions to triggers that provoke your insecurities and make you feel like defending yourself. During such events, your attention immediately goes to those who triggered you, instead of going inward to understand why you're triggered.

Of course, your goal is noble. Your defense is justifiable. You want them to go away and never trigger you again. Yet no matter what you employ as a defensive action, they keep coming back, because you never solve the puzzle of who your Vulnerable Self is and why it keeps taking these triggers personally. Without such self-knowledge, you keep facing these intense trigger events and feel stuck and lost in these never-ending drama cycles.

For over a decade and a half, I've witnessed clients break free from these drama cycles after acquiring a particular, sensitive self-knowledge from these trigger events. The task is not easy, but it is doable as you become more aware of who your Vulnerable Self is. After all, that's why you take these situations personally. If you didn't have any Vulnerable Self, your life would be filled with joy and happiness, as no one could trigger you.

You need to go to the source, the moment when you're triggered. That's exactly when your Vulnerable Self becomes active. What you're defending with your emotional reactions is your insecurities, your vulnerabilities. I know, and I hope you now understand, that in those moments, the last thing you want to see is your Vulnerable Self, as you desperately want to hide this little brother. Deep down, you actually want to avoid the current experience because it seems too similar to what you experienced in your past.

During a trigger event, what's really happening is that others are simply triggering the feelings that have been kept unprocessed in your subconscious. Since these unprocessed feelings stay raw in your psyche as if they happened yesterday (your subconscious doesn't have a sense of time), the triggers make you feel the same emotional hurt, almost exactly what you experienced before.

Taking a deeper look at how a drama cycle unfolds helps expand your self-awareness and gives you the opportunity to acquire that immensely valuable self-knowledge about your Vulnerable Self.

First, the cycle kicks off with a trigger event. Either a person or a situation, or at times your own negative inner talk, creates an emotional reaction in you. As soon as your Vulnerable Self feels insecure, an emotional charge, such as anger, frustration, sadness, anxiety, and so on is created. The word *emotion* actually means "energy in motion", e-motion. Your subconscious uses this energy, this charge for you to take a defensive, fight-or-flight stance against the trigger.

When your body is charged with such powerful electricity, you apply all sorts of defensive actions to deal with triggers. In the process of defending yourself, you end up exhausting your energy by yelling or throwing things around or rolling your eyes or gossiping about people or running out of the room or ignoring others. All of these reactions cost you enormous energy. At the end, you suppress your vulnerability and everything you feel.

No matter what you do, these fight-or-flight defensive actions don't seem to yield any positive outcomes. As a result, you end up feeling exhausted and also stuck in these never ending drama cycles, perpetuating your mental and emotional suffering. Since your defensive reactions bring you to these devastating results, how about changing things up, and looking beneath your emotions and understanding why you emotionally react in the first place?

Did you know that your emotions are actually created by your thoughts? Yes, a situation becomes a trigger event, and elicits emotional reaction in you, only because your subconscious interprets the situation as a threat to your vulnerability. As a result, it makes you "think" that this situation is an insult to your conditioned persona, which kicks off your fight-or-flight defense mechanism, which then creates enough emotional charge to help you defend yourself.

As you can imagine, your subconscious programming cannot be easily accessed, but you'll be able to decode it through paying attention to your perceptions, as they appear as thoughts in your mind at the time of the trigger event. At the end of the day, your emotions are only there because of your thoughts. Since your thoughts are only there because of your perceptions, you want to understand what influences your perceptions. In other words, where do your thoughts come from?

They appear from your feelings. A feeling is an internal impression of how a trigger event affects you. Back to our original example: When parents demand all A's, and the kid fails with two B's on their scorecard, they feel not good enough. They feel like a failure. What happens to those feelings? The kid is not aware of them. Therefore, they stay unprocessed in the subconscious. Decades later, what happens when that person's current boss criticizes them for failing to put a not-so-important detail in a report? Their unprocessed feelings of not being good enough and being a failure are provoked again, as if their parents are criticizing them.

That's how unprocessed feelings trigger the thoughts, which trigger the emotional reactions. When you subconsciously keep defensively reacting to the trigger events, what happens to these unprocessed feelings over time? They turn into repressed fears. Your subconscious infiltrates them into the thought patterns, belief systems, and values of your Vulnerable Self. This subconscious process reinforces a sense of identity, a persona that you're indeed not good enough, never recognized, always devalued, and so on.

You see how these drama cycles carry so much information about your Vulnerable Self and why you react to trigger events the way you do. By closely observing those times you are triggered, you can acquire profound insights about your Vulnerable Self and identify what your repressed fears are. When you thoroughly understand and realize why you take these triggers so personally, this self-knowledge eventually sets you free from drama cycles.

BIRTH OF THE CONDITIONED SELF

These trigger events are mentally and emotionally damaging and physically draining. It's impossible to live in such a fearful, unsafe, and unpredictable state of mind. As a result, your subconscious steps in and gives birth to your Conditioned Self, whose goal is to be the protective shield, the mask that disguises the repressed fears and hides the Vulnerable Self from others.

The creation of the Conditioned Self is a reactive process. Without your conscious awareness, you begin to act precisely according to the programming that developed in the name of protecting your vulnerability; this becomes your persona. When you act out your conditioned personas, you pay too much attention to others to sense if they pose any possible threats to your vulnerability. Therefore, with your attention constantly outward, it becomes extremely difficult to spot your Conditioned Self in action and understand why you do the things the way you do.

Let's look through some examples of the Conditioned Self together and see if some of these prominent personas resonate with you as potential masks you wear in your life today.

Adventure Seeker: Do you feel like you don't have enough personal space and yearn to explore vast lands with open-ended travel plans? Do you sense that your life is limited by what you do and how many people you interact with, and that you need more from life? Do you think you can do more than you currently do, and that you are called to bigger and better experiences in the world?

Apologist: Do you constantly say "Sorry"? Do you use a soft, quiet voice and try not to offend anyone? Do you easily and immediately take the blame when something goes wrong?

Approval Seeker: Do you find it difficult to make your own decisions, whether they're minor or major, and feel that you need to get others' opinions before doing so? Do you change your behavior, attitude, tone, or mood depending on the person you're interacting with and ask for their assurance that you're doing something right? Do you worry about how you're perceived by others and if you're going to get judged for your actions or behavior?

Attention Seeker: Do you want all eyes on you? Do you engage in specific behaviors to make yourself the focus of others' attention and admiration? Do you get bored or pouty when people talk to others and not to you?

Boss: Do you always know the best way to do things and don't care much about what others think? Do you value your ability to tell others what to do over feeling curious about their ideas, suggestions, or opinions? Do you feel that you're naturally better at leading and continually feel frustrated when others don't simply follow your guidance?

Bully: Do you make fun of people and justify it as a joke? Do you demean or belittle people with humiliating, humorous, or sarcastic comments and gestures? Do you feel threatened when someone challenges your boundaries and react aggressively to them with yelling or condescending behavior?

Caregiver: Do you spend too much time taking care of others and never have enough time for yourself? Do you feel tired, exhausted, or irritable; sleep too much or not enough; or are you too sensitive in your interactions due to giving everything you have to others? Do you struggle to find time to spend on things that bring you joy and feel guilty if you're having fun while others are suffering?

Chronically Late: Do you find yourself always running late to meetings, whether they are important or not, and always feel embarrassed and out of control? Do you feel like there's not enough time for everything, so you try to squeeze in "just one more thing" while forgetting about your time-bound obligations? Do you feel your time is so limited and so valuable that you try to arrive right on time or even a few minutes late rather than being there five minutes early and waiting for others?

Conflict Avoider: Do you withdraw from possible confrontations with others and passively agree just to avoid any escalation of conflict? Do you find yourself changing the topic of conversation for the sake of keeping the peace at home, at work, or among friends and forgo the need to address the issue or find a reasonable solution to the problem at hand? Do you find it irritating or annoying that people constantly argue, and do you leave or stay anxiously quiet when you're in proximity to conflict?

Controller: Do you have the urge to be in charge in every situation and take care of everything that is going on? Do you direct others on what to do and how to do it, and get sulky, withdrawn, bitter, or judgmental when things don't go the way you want? Do you criticize others for making mistakes and micromanage them so they don't repeat their errors in the future, or so you feel more comfortable with their performance?

Doubter: Do you always see the downside of things? Do you lack trust in people, situations, or life in general? Are you always skeptical and withdrawn, and do you doubt that anything will change for the better in your life?

Escapist: Do you feel like the world is a bad place that you need to isolate yourself from? Do you lean in to religious, spiritual, agnostic, or philosophical groups and communities to find your tribe? Do you get lost in your dreams, wishes, and fantasies so you can avoid thinking about the unpleasantries of life, or obsessively watch TV, surf the internet, or scroll on social media so you can tune things out?

Fixer: Do you try to make sure everyone around you is happy and try to make them feel better if they're not? Do you tend to immediately go into fixing mode when someone asks you a question about something they're struggling with? Do you instantly make yourself available to your family and friends when they face a conflict or a challenge?

High Achiever: Do you feel like you always have to be the best at whatever you do? Do you feel like your competitive spirit keeps you motivated during difficult tasks and lifts you up in moments of disappointment and failure? Do you take pleasure in reaching your goals, and to support that, you stay ambitious, goal-oriented, and self-disciplined to accomplish as much as you can?

Loner: Are you an individualist who enjoys your time alone? Do you sense needing alone time not necessarily because you don't like people, but rather because you prefer living in your own world and in your own thoughts? Do you regain energy from spending time on your own, so you don't actively seek out interactions with others?

Multitasker: Do you get satisfaction from tackling more than one thing at a time and get a sense of gratification when they're all done? Do you feel like you have to be efficient all the time so you pack a lot in? Do you feel like your to-do list just keeps growing and there's always something in the way of getting everything done?

Penny-Pincher: Do you always think about how much things cost and try to minimize the money you spend while maximizing the experience? Do you feel like you're the only one who understands the value of money and worries about expenses? Do you get innate satisfaction from buying things on sale, finding the best deal, or using coupons to receive discounts?

People Pleaser: Do you put others' needs ahead of yours and cater to what you think they need at the expense of your own needs? Do you have a deep sensitivity to what others expect from you and feel you always need to be agreeable, helpful, and kind to meet their expectations? Do you find yourself locked in patterns of self-sacrifice and self-neglect and feel like it's hard to stand up for your rights and boundaries?

Perfectionist: Do you strive to make your environment immaculate and orderly? Do you expect your family life, work life, financial systems, and political systems to be flawless, fair, and just? And do you expect people and situations to meet your high standards of moral code, performance, and action?

Positive Thinker: Do you feel like you are almost always the cheerful and optimistic one? Do you avoid unpleasant situations and difficult people because they bring negativity into your life? Do you always believe in the best possible result and hope for it to manifest even if it is not likely to happen?

Procrastinator: Do you find yourself unnecessarily delaying or postponing projects, even though you know there will be negative consequences if you do? Do you have stagnant, tired, and unmotivated energy that makes you put things off, like house projects, work deadlines, household chores, paying the bills, or submitting taxes? Do you always say you will start things tomorrow instead of starting today, like beginning a diet, quitting smoking, watching less TV, or waking up early?

Social Butterfly: Are you a socially dynamic person who loves meeting people, is great at networking, and knows a lot of people from many diverse groups? At parties and social gatherings you attend, do you have the urge to talk to everyone, so you jump from person to person, staying in touch with almost everybody? Do you get compliments about how easygoing you are, how easy to talk to, how outgoing, gregarious, vibrant, energetic, and popular you are?

Know-It-All: Do you act like you know how to do everything and have specific thoughts and opinions about how things should be done? Do you like hearing yourself talk and pride yourself on how knowledgeable you are, and do you dismiss others' opinions, suggestions, and thoughts because they are uninformed? Do you, from time to time, encounter people who tell you that you're self-centered or get into arguments with them because you're sure that you're right?

Traditionalist: Are you set in your own ways and refuse to consider new ways of living or thinking about life? Do you gain a sense of security when things stay the way they are, and you don't want to change things if they're working fine? Do others call you conservative and challenge you to consider the way you think about or do things, yet you find those challenges offensive and unnecessary interventions into your accustomed way of living?

Thrill Chaser: Do you find yourself doing or fantasizing about daring activities like jumping out of planes, solo rock climbing, surfing Mavericks, or completing hundred-mile runs? Do you feel like ordinary life is too stagnant and there's no purpose in living in confined terms? Do you get agitated whenever you have to do a mundane task or conform with rules and norms?

Victim: Do you feel like a victim in situations where you are put down, excluded, dismissed? Do you believe that all the bad situations happen to you? Are you easily and naturally intimidated by others?

Worrier: Are you always worrying about things when worry is not warranted, and later on it turns out not to be a big deal? Do you obsessively think about possible risks, dangers, and worst-case scenarios, while others don't seem to care too much about those things? Do you act on your worries and check to make sure that everything is prepared for possible disaster, yet the worries and anxious thoughts never leave you, and you constantly take more cautious actions?

Note that these masks are neither good nor bad. They are just character traits that protect your vulnerability and hide your insecurities. However, without consciously realizing, you keep wearing the same mask and playing the same role. What happens then? You subconsciously create a safe border, a comfort zone, and stay within your conditioned behavior.

This defensive and protective approach doesn't allow you to explore life beyond your comfort zone. You then miss out on experiencing a fulfilling life. You keep doing what feels familiar and what you are conditioned for.

No matter how much you hide behind these masks though, others keep creating drama cycles by triggering you and making you feel vulnerable, insecure, unhappy, and unfulfilled. No matter what you do, how you react to others, or how many times you tell them not to repeat certain things, you continue to be exposed to these triggers. The reason for such experiences is simply due to your unprocessed feelings and repressed fears that foster the actions of your Conditioned Self.

1ST TRANSFORMATION STRATEGY: PAUSING AND OBSERVING YOUR SELF IN ACTION

You can imagine how difficult it is to catch your Conditioned Self in action. Yet that's the goal of this first phase: to spot the mask you wear exactly when you're wearing it. Can you remember today, tonight, tomorrow to pay attention to what kind of persona you're playing in your interactions?

To execute this tall order, you need to be able to pause and observe your conditioned actions from a distance, which is your first transformation strategy. When you get lost in your persona, asking the following questions could help you remember to take a step back and quietly observe your Conditioned Self:

- What mask am I wearing right now?
- What is the motivation behind my actions?
- What am I trying to accomplish here?

The key to successfully executing the first transformation strategy is to remember that in any given moment you're playing your Conditioned Self. Here is the difficulty: who's going to pause to ask these questions and then observe your conditioned behavior to identify the masks you're currently wearing?

To accomplish this task, you need to create an outside observer, an independent witness who can watch your Conditioned Self without compromising the quality of your interactions with others.

Naturally, the next question is, how can you create this outside witness who's not your Conditioned Self but the observer of its masks? You need a so-called self-observation practice that trains you to manage your attention. By consciously getting hold of your attention, you slowly develop this outside observer of your conditioned behavior and spot your Conditioned Self, no matter how immersed you are while interacting with others.

1ST TRANSFORMATION TECHNIQUE: PRACTICING SELF-OBSERVATION MEDITATION

Even though it's called meditation, this self-observation practice is neither to quiet your mind nor achieve some kind of inner calmness. Its purpose is simpler: just be aware of when you're lost in your thoughts or in your conditioned behavior. When you practice Self-Observation Meditation on a daily basis, your attention will be so sharp that you sense a palpable mental space between you (the observer) and your Conditioned Self.

That mental space feels like a gap between you and your thoughts. In that space, you can manage to be the outside observer and remain detached and removed from your conditioned behavior. When that happens, you feel unhooked from the reins of your subconscious and maintain a neutral and objective presence in the midst of any interaction.

With more and more practice as the outside observer, you become completely independent from your conditioned behavior; you develop the inner strength to pause and observe what's going on outside of yourself and notice all the subtleties that go on within your mind, heart, and body.

Here's how you practice Self-Observation Meditation:

First, pick a location where you won't be interrupted. I suggest you start with a three-minute practice as a beginner. When you're more comfortable with how it's done, you can add more time.

To start, sit on a comfortable chair with your knees at a ninety-degree angle and your feet flat on the floor. Your back, neck, and head are straight. If the chair has a back, scoot forward toward the center of the seat so you're not leaning backward. If you have to support yourself on the back of the chair, that's okay too, but keep your spine straight. Relax your body and maintain this posture without becoming too rigid or strained.

Now, put your hands on your lap, facing up. Place your right fingers underneath your left fingers. Make sure they lie on top of each other without interlocking. Your fingers, along with your upward facing palms, form a nice cradle. Let your thumbs softly touch each other, creating an arch, a round shape over your palms.

With your arms relaxed, thumbs lightly touching, take a deep breath in and close your eyes on the exhale. Put the tip of your tongue behind your front teeth and place your tongue gently on the roof of your mouth. Keep your mouth closed, breathing naturally.

Then, start concentrating on your thumbs and focus on the tangible feeling where they touch. While trying to keep your focus on that sensation, gently observe the thoughts and images that are going through your mind. Whenever you find yourself getting lost in your thoughts, bring your attention back to your thumbs. Notice what you're thinking without reacting or making judgments. Just note what you're thinking with calm indifference and detachment.

In the beginning, you will find that you are constantly distracted by your thoughts. You'll lose your concentration and start thinking about memories, regrets, and future concerns. Whenever you find your thoughts wandering, pause and ask yourself, "What am I thinking right now?" This question will create a brief pause where you will be able to acknowledge your thoughts and become the observer again. Then, slowly and patiently, bring your focus back to your thumbs.

As you practice, let your observer notice this tug-of-war between the chatter in your mind and your concentration. The goal is to keep your attention on your thumbs for increasingly longer periods of time. But don't get frustrated if you can't hold your focus for more than a few seconds at first. That is okay. You are not trying to overcome your mind chatter or make it stop. Instead, you are trying to observe it so that you can create a mental space between you and your thoughts, where the objective observer can naturally emerge.

To finish your practice, take a deep breath and exhale slowly. Then open your eyes and release your hands. Sit quietly for a minute or two to reflect on any repeating thoughts or images you encountered during your practice and notice how it felt to observe them from the outside.

I highly recommend practicing the Self-Observation Meditation for three minutes every morning, right after you wake up. If you're comfortable with it, you can also repeat the exercise every night before you go to bed. Once you're more familiar with the technique, add more minutes to your practice and do it at different times throughout your day.

REAL LIFE SCENARIO

Anna was a high achiever, blindly chasing success, asking for early promotions, and seeking instant gratifications. She didn't want to waste any time being idle. Her life was passing by. For her, life meant a busy schedule—a calendar filled with back-to-back meetings and constant sports activities, dinner dates, and jazz nights. She found meaning in this stressful busy-ness of her life. She felt this was her purpose, to live life fully, without any moment of rest or reflection.

However, deep down, when she allowed herself to "feel," she was surprised that no matter how hard she worked, she always felt unrecognized for her efforts. She felt that in meetings, her ideas were not being acknowledged or appreciated as much as others'. At night, when she put her head onto her pillow, she compared herself to others, to her colleagues, and thought how much she was failing, or falling short of higher achievements.

Her background was filled with glorious achievements. She went to great schools but always felt like an impostor. She knew there were smarter people than her who accomplished more than she was able to. One day, she realizes what she had unintentionally done to herself. She basically got herself onto a hamster wheel, which kept her running, running for her life, and keeping her under its hegemony, its control, slowly taking her energy away and making her feel tired, exhausted, and drained all the time.

Upon this realization, she decides to get off this hamster wheel that makes her life miserable despite all the success she accomplished so far. She immediately goes to a local Barnes & Noble bookstore, and gets hold of as many self-help books as she can. She starts reading and learning about human psyche and conditioning. She looks up personal growth seminars and starts attending them.

Slowly, she becomes more aware of her Self. She realizes she's running on an internal programming, called "high achiever." She reflects on her conditioning. Everything she does has the motivation of achieving higher levels of success. That realization makes her recognize how she's lost her joy for life, as it all became a pile of to-do lists and goals to climb higher and higher.

Such deep insights motivate her to change her conditioned behavior. She starts to meditate and deliberately observe her frantic, highly energized personality designed for success. As she digs deeper, she finds the ability and the power to consciously slow down. She becomes more mindful of her time and where she spends it. This awareness brings more actions of self-care and self-respect. Until that time, she has never realized that seeking validation from others is a form of self-disrespect.

The newly found goal of respecting her time and personal space leads her to carve out more breathing room in her life and eventually leads her to recover from her chronic fatigue she has been feeling for years. For some reason, maybe her ability to manage her stress, as well as her busy calendar, she feels healthier and more robust in her body as her energy expands.

As a by-product of her becoming more self-aware, Anna starts to get more connected with her husband as she now has more energy, motivation, and willingness to share herself with him. Naturally, she becomes more open to do things together. As her mood lights up, her eating habits get healthier, her skin shines, she becomes more confident and comfortable. Most shockingly though, she starts to receive more recognition at work as her productivity and efficiency soar as a direct result of her positive energy.

PHASE 1 REFLECTIONS

Since your goal in this first phase is to become aware of your Conditioned Self, your primary directive is to be that outside observer of your conditioned behavior. To develop that independent observer, you need mental space. Once you create that gap between you, your thoughts, and your conditioned behavior, it'll be easier to pause and observe how your Conditioned Self shows up in your life.

For the next seven days, make a journal entry at the end of each day and write down your answers to the following questions:

1. How difficult is it to pause and observe your Conditioned Self?

2. How was your experience with Self-Observation Meditation today?

3. How does your morning practice influence your mood during the day?

4. What kind of masks do you notice in your daily interactions?

5. What kind of unprocessed feelings are you able to identify when triggered?

PHASE 2

UNDERSTANDING YOUR CONDITIONED SELF

The second phase of your personal transformation journey is an invitation for a detailed review of your life. Once you start to observe your Conditioned Self from afar, you may naturally feel curious to go deeper and discover what lies behind those conditioned behaviors. By learning how to reflect on your past experiences, you slowly start to understand how you formed these particular masks and why your subconscious adopted them as protective shields and survival mechanisms.

As you know by now, your Conditioned Self exists only to hide your vulnerability, in other words, your repressed fears. These fears are basically the unprocessed feelings that are withheld, suppressed, or ignored during emotionally traumatic events in your past.

To avoid extreme emotional pain, your subconscious created your masks and their conditioned behaviors, pretending as if nothing happened. As a result, you bypassed processing your feelings and associated repressed fears. They remained untouched in your subconscious and continued influencing your perceptions (your thoughts, beliefs, and values), keeping you in a state of fear and anxiety. That's why a trigger event can affect you emotionally.

The good news is that no matter how much your subconscious tries to hide your repressed fears, you keep getting exposed to trigger events, giving you the opportunity to discover the very vulnerability your subconscious is trying to hide. While these triggers may seem like personal attacks, try to treat them like mirrors—opportunities for you to see your masks reflect your insecurities back at you.

For example, let's say that one day your boss criticizes your job performance and tells you that the quality of your work is disappointing. A week later, your spouse compares you unfavorably to your friend. And then a few months later, someone at work receives an award or gets promoted to a position that you felt you deserved. All these situations, while independent of each other, could trigger your repressed fears and make you feel "inadequate," "unrecognized," or "unvalued," depending on how your unique past experiences have shaped your subconscious programming.

Your typical emotional reaction might be to get angry or frustrated with your boss or spouse, or feel jealous that someone else got recognition instead of you. Then your defense mechanisms might be to vent to your friends about the unfairness of your boss, get into an argument with your spouse, or choose not to talk to your promoted colleague for a while.

But when you take these defensive actions, you don't really process your repressed fears, which are the root cause of your emotional reactions. You simply remain unaware of your insecurities. They stay buried in your subconscious and become heavier and heavier. They drag your mood down. The lower your mood is, the snappier you get. The more irritable you get, the longer you stay in the drama cycles, exhausting your energy to defend your vulnerability.

Since emotional reactions don't process the heaviness of your repressed fears, you give in to addictions to numb your emotional pain. Such actions, like overeating, watching too much TV, drinking excessively, and so on, are the tell-tale signs of mental and emotional suffering caused by your unprocessed feelings and repressed fears. With these coping mechanisms, all you really want to do is comfort yourself and forget about your emotional wounds. But you can't keep running away from triggers and hiding behind the masks of your Conditioned Self.

FOCUSING ON EMOTIONAL REACTIONS

Why do you keep emotionally reacting to people?

Because of your perceptions. People are perceived as a threat to your safety, your character, or your values.

Who is getting really triggered?

Your Conditioned Self, in other words, it's your protective persona that is designed to hide your vulnerability is the one who's getting triggered.

Why does a trigger become a threat?

Because it challenges the insecurities of your Vulnerable Self and challenges the safety and security you built around your unprocessed feelings, i.e., repressed fears.

That's why these people, these trigger events, feel so insulting to you. As a result, you take them personally. Every trigger elicits an emotional reaction from you because it touches your vulnerability by prodding your repressed fears. You react because they seemingly confirm what you subconsciously fear deep inside.

For example, let's say your repressed fear is not being good enough. When someone criticizes you, your Conditioned Self perceives that they're confirming that you are not good enough. Your repressed fear is now afflicted, and you are offended. You take their criticism personally. Then you get angry and emotionally react to them for making you feel that way. Think about it. In this scenario, would you have reacted to them for their criticism if you didn't have the repressed fear of "not being good enough"?

Your emotional reactions are the tip of the iceberg. Under the surface, they carry an enormous amount of information, which is completely programmed by your subconscious. This programming basically consists of your conditioned thought patterns, belief systems, and values.

Let's use this criticism as an example to see what's going on internally in your subconscious before you show an emotional reaction.

1. **The trigger happens.** Someone criticizes you.

2. **Your repressed fears are triggered.** Subconsciously, this criticism—maybe even their attitude, their tone of voice, the way they looked at you, or the type of criticism they made—reminds you of situations where a parent might have made similar comments that made you feel not good enough, which eventually became your repressed fear.

3. **Your feelings are provoked.** This elicits past feelings of not being good enough, like in the past emotionally hurtful experiences with your parent.

4. **Your thoughts interpret the situation according to your feelings and repressed fears of not being good enough.** You think the person who criticized you is implying exactly what you experienced in the past, confirming that you're not good enough.

5. **Your emotions are activated.** You're now angry at the person who's criticizing you and making you feel vulnerable and insecure, which you subconsciously try to hide. You're now exposed, and your fight-or-flight defense mechanisms take over the situation and emotionally react to the person to ward off the threat.

To understand your Conditioned Self, you need to be able to reverse engineer your emotions all the way to your repressed fears.

IDENTIFYING YOUR REPRESSED FEARS

The key to breaking free from this old life and creating a new one is to process these repressed fears. But do you know what they are? What are your possible repressed fears? Let's see which one(s) of these repressed fears you identify with in the table below.

While reading through the table, put "I feel _____" in front of each one. "I feel abandoned," or "I feel criticized," and so on, and see which statements resonate with you.

- Abandoned
- Belittled
- Betrayed
- Bullied
- Cheated
- Controlled
- Criticized
- Devalued
- Disapproved of
- Dismissed
- Disregarded

- Financially Unstable
- Inadequate
- Intimidated
- Judged
- Like a Failure
- Like an Impostor
- Lonely
- Manipulated
- Misunderstood
- Neglected
- Not Good Enough

- Put Down
- Rejected
- Taken for Granted
- Trapped
- Unappreciated
- Unheard
- Unrecognized
- Unseen
- Unworthy
- Used

Please note that this list represents the most common repressed fears I've encountered in my practice. While other unlisted fears may resonate with you, trust your intuition to identify what feels most relevant to your experience.

How does this self-knowledge prevent you from getting triggered?

The answer to this very important question lies in the deep connection between your repressed fears and the Conditioned Self.

Let's expand on what we discussed earlier. As you now know repressed fears represent your vulnerability. Your subconscious suppresses them to hide your insecurities from others. This act of disguise creates a passive force, which is your Vulnerable Self. Your subconscious then compensates for these repressed fears with hidden desires, forming the active force that creates your Conditioned Self – the mask that hides your vulnerability.

In other words, your repressed fears make you take conservative actions to stay in your comfort zone, while your hidden desires are the opposing force that drive you to go against those fears.

For example, if you have a fear of "not being recognized," your Conditioned Self will most likely wear the mask of a high achiever with a hidden desire of "being recognized." Now imagine yourself doing things to receive recognition from others. You're forcing your agenda. In that case, how likely do you think people will grant you the recognition that you desperately need? The chances are slim, and you're more likely be exposed to triggers, the harder you try to get recognized.

Throughout the Journey Within process, your main goal is to identify your repressed fears and hidden desires and neutralize them to bring their opposing passive and active forces into an equal state, which then allows you to consciously override your automatic subconscious tendencies and as a result, avoid future triggers.

UNDERSTANDING THE ORIGINS OF YOUR CONDITIONED SELF

Remember, your subconscious works to protect you from experiencing the emotional wounds of past traumatic events. From the moment you experience hurt, your subconscious creates different forces that govern the actions of your mind and body, ultimately leading to the development of your Conditioned Self.

Original Trigger Event → Repressed Fear → Hidden Desires → Conditioned Self

The question then becomes: how can you determine which emotionally wounding traumatic event led your subconscious to create your Conditioned Self?

The following steps will guide you through the process.

1. Apply the self-observation practice to every possible moment to pause and observe your actions in real time to identify what masks your Conditioned Self wears.

2. Once you notice what kind of conditioned actions you take, look more deeply at what motivates your actions. What are your hidden desires?

3. Then, what are the repressed fears that your conditioned actions are trying to hide? What is the opposite of your hidden desires?

4. Finally, recall the events from your past that made you behave in similar ways.

Helen, one of my clients, was a social butterfly. Her hidden desire was to connect with as many people as possible. She didn't care about how close or how deep these connections were, as long as she could call them "friends." Why social butterfly? In her case, she was trying to hide her repressed fear of abandonment. The original trigger event happened when her small, close-knit circle of friends in high school joined the popular clique and left her behind. It was a big shock to her, as she valued their friendships. They were a very closely knit group, and did everything together, until they didn't, when they broke up.

Helen felt abandoned. She cried for days. She was ashamed to go to school, because she felt she was not wanted. She wasn't the chosen one, the other people were. Her subconscious had to go to work and program a hidden desire for her to make more friends. She didn't care if they were close. She was going merely for the numbers. The more friends she had, the better she felt, even though those friends were not so deep.

After all, she didn't want to make the same mistake and rely on a small number of close friends and deep connections that could potentially leave her alone one day. She wanted to hedge the risk of being abandoned, even with superficial connections. As a result, her mask, her Conditioned Self, became a social butterfly.

It was a miserable year for her. Luckily, her parents moved to another neighborhood and registered her at a new school. Next school year, she was able to apply her new conditioned behavior and made a lot of friends. Even though her subconscious and her conditioned behavior hedged the risk of being abandoned, her repressed fears always made her feel cautious any time one of those friends became closer to her. Without realizing, she kept pushing them away, and never let them come close.

Isn't that interesting? Can you relate to her? Like her, when you reflect on your past and understand how your repressed fears are formed, you can sense your hidden desires behind your conditioned actions. Once you connect with that force, you're better able to relate to your Conditioned Self in a more intimate way. You can then truly understand why you do the things the way you do and connect with what really makes you who you are today.

Before we dive into strategies and techniques to deeply understand how your Conditioned Self is formed in the first place, let's look at some examples of possible emotional wounds that you might be carrying behind your masks and how those vulnerabilities and insecurities influence your conditioned actions today.

EXAMPLE 1:
CONDITIONED SELF: PERFECTIONIST

You want to excel in everything you do and exhaust yourself with effort. You try hard to be a good citizen and do what's required of you, but if you fail, you become extremely self-critical and demeaning toward yourself. You harbor anger toward others who are laid back and don't care about being good or following the rules. Since you want to be the best and not be judged for being bad, you may become a workaholic, or you may act overly proper or reserved to prevent yourself from making mistakes. You may also have a controlling personality with a strong need to feel everything is under your control.

> **Hidden Desire:** You want to prove that you are good enough and that things can be perfect if you put in the work.
>
> **Repressed Fear:** Fear of not being good enough.

Original Trigger Event: You might have had very strict parents; your dad was a disciplinarian, and your mom was controlling. You were not allowed to make mistakes and everything you did was closely monitored. If you received praise, it was a few brief words, followed by instructions on how to be better next time.

EXAMPLE 2: CONDITIONED SELF: HIGH ACHIEVER

You dream big and are ambitious. You connect with life through your work. It doesn't matter what you do; you aim for the stars. You accomplish many things, but you're always hungry for more. You are imaginative and creative. You always have grand plans and strategies to accomplish things with energy and fire. You draw people into your life and connect with them with your liveliness and energy.

Hidden Desire: You want the satisfaction of accomplishing things and being recognized to feel the emotional connection that you missed early on in your life.

Repressed Fear: Fear of not being recognized.

Original Trigger Event: Your dad might have been distant and aloof, and he didn't care about your accomplishments or other aspects of your life. Your mom was also emotionally unavailable and never saw you for who you were. You constantly felt alone. Neither of your parents could relate to you, and as a result, you never learned how to connect emotionally with other people.

EXAMPLE 3: CONDITIONED SELF: CAREGIVER

You attend to others' needs and prioritize them over your own. You may play the role of savior or organizer for people in need of your help and care. You can't help but impulsively jump in to lend a hand when someone is having a hard time, but you give so much of yourself that sometimes you feel resentful. You also feel as though no one understands you well enough to be willing to step up and help you when you need something once in a blue moon.

Hidden Desire: You probably still feel resentment, which comes out toward people who ignore your help or efforts for connection, but you keep hoping to feel included by them and to receive praise, compliments, and acknowledgment for the care you show them.

Repressed Fear: Fear of not being valued; fear of being rejected, dismissed.

Original Trigger Event: Your parents may have been so busy with work or parental obligations that they didn't pay much attention to you. Or you may have been raised by a grandparent. Later on, when your younger sibling was born, you worked hard at home to help your mom. However, no matter what you did to make your mom happy, she never expressed any verbal appreciation for your efforts and didn't attend to your needs for emotional intimacy. You kept helping in the hope that one day she'd see you and appreciate your efforts, but that appreciation never came, and you left home right after high school carrying a lot of resentment about how your contributions to the family were overlooked.

Now, following the above format, can you pause here and spend some time creating a similar template for the specific masks that you identified earlier as your Conditioned Self? In the following strategy and technique for this chapter, I'll help you fill in the blanks around the original trigger event.

2ND TRANSFORMATION STRATEGY: CONNECTING WITH YOUR PAST

You may have a hard time remembering what happened in your past. Even if you can identify the specific mask you wear, it may still be difficult for you to trace it to the original trigger event. Even if you can't identify it immediately, keep observing your Conditioned Self in action and take notes of what is happening within yourself. Don't push too hard to identify something specific from your past.

Instead, double down on your Self-Observation Meditation. This practice expands your mind and frees it up from the existing noise that blocks clear and critical thinking that gives you access to your past experiences. The clearer your mind becomes, the easier it is for you to connect with memories you have long forgotten. Most of my clients have interesting memories pop up out of the blue, like when they're brushing their teeth, walking on the street, shopping at the grocery store, driving to work, or dreaming.

While waiting for memories to come up naturally, you can also reach out to your parents, relatives, cousins, and childhood friends and ask them questions about how you acted as a child, how your family structure was, and how your interactions were while growing up. During this process, some of my clients discover their diaries from their teenage years, which is always a fun read. If you kept a personal journal or diary like them, see if you can locate it, as they make excellent reference to your past experiences and how you felt about them.

To help you with this process, here are a few questions you can use:
- What was the relationship like between your parents?
- What is their view on life?
- What is their life story? How did they meet?
- What was their lifestyle before and after you were born?
- How did your parents treat you?
- What was your upbringing like?
- What were the family dynamics between you and your parents and you and your siblings?
- What kind of thoughts and beliefs were imposed on you by your parents, siblings, friends, and teachers?
- What were your parents' expectations of you?
- How did you fit into the family?
- How did your teachers treat you?
- How were your interactions with your friends or classmates?
- What did you think about your life growing up?

To make this process go smoothly, obtain a natural curiosity by imagining that you are a detective, investigating your own life with empathy, compassion, and understanding—but also with detachment. Try not to analyze the events you learn about. Don't try to discover why your parents or other people treated you the way they did. Try not to justify their actions. Don't worry about making sense of their behaviors. Purely focus on how you felt at the time and what you thought about these specific situations.

You may experience some emotional pain by opening old wounds. Looking back and reliving the painful memories you tried to forget is not pleasant. Facing the feelings of inferiority, insecurity, isolation, and more is not comfortable. However, understanding your past to create a new future is worth the exercise. Every original trigger event you uncover sheds so much light on your current life that you start feeling lighter and lighter. The deeper you go, the easier it becomes to stay on the path to self-realization and turn the corner for a more joyful and fulfilling life.

2ND TRANSFORMATION TECHNIQUE: REVERSE ENGINEERING WITH "WHAT IF, SO WHAT"

In addition to investigating your past, how can you discover the origins of your repressed fears and understand why your subconscious formed your Conditioned Self to hide them?

We said earlier that your repressed fears often come from childhood interactions with your parents, the environment you grew up in, the community you belonged to, the schools you attended, or the friend groups you hung out with. But you are exposed to so many different experiences throughout your life; how can you possibly know which ones still affect you in everyday life today?

The answers are buried in your subconscious. You can't really reference outside resources, books, teachers, or teachings to learn exactly why and how your subconscious created masks to hide your repressed fears. The only way to learn about them is to decipher the subconscious programming that you operate under. The process of deeper understanding of these conditioned actions requires reverse engineering.

How do you use reverse engineering? You use it when you have an emotional reaction to a trigger. That's exactly when you start reverse engineering the thoughts that created your emotions. In a sense, it's a process of internal investigation of your conditioned mental structure by challenging it with a series of "What If, So What" questions.

Let's say Ken dismisses his wife, Maryann's idea on a house project that he had been working on for a while. But later on, she realizes that he accepted neighbor Bob's idea, which was similar to what Maryann suggested in the first place.

Now, if it were you, how would you react to your spouse? Well, Maryann gets pissed off. She can't believe that Ken would ignore her. Well, it's probably not the first time her ideas have been brushed aside while someone else's are accepted. But nonetheless, Maryann can't help but think that Ken constantly dismisses her and what she has to say, because he gives more credit to others and thinks their opinions are more important than hers.

Let's start reverse engineering with Maryann's first thought: "Ken dismissed my idea! Again!" Now, she would challenge that thought with a "What If, So What" question. The following is her internal dialogue:

> Q: What if Ken dismissed my idea? So what?

> A: He always ignores me. He's always dismissive in our interactions. Nothing is new.

> *(This answer doesn't tell her much about her feelings. So, she tries another "What If, So What" question to challenge her last thought.)*

> Q: What if he ignores me? So what?

> A: I feel like my opinions don't matter to him. He never values me. He never listens to what I have to say.

(Again, Maryann challenges her last thought with "What If, So What.")

Q: What if Ken never values me and never listens to me? So what? How does that make me feel?

A: I'll feel dismissed, not valued, and not recognized.

She can stop here and identify these as her repressed fears. These are very likely familiar feelings that Maryann has experienced throughout her life.

You may naturally wonder how many repressed fears you carry within your psyche. Through my work with thousands of clients, I've realized we have three to five major repressed fears. They are the culprits for our emotional reactions. You now know that as long as these repressed fears remain unprocessed, you'll keep experiencing trigger events. The contrary is also true: where you identify your repressed fears with "What If, So What" questions and take action to process them, you'll start to feel glimpses of hope that there is a way to break free from the negative drama cycles.

REAL LIFE SCENARIO

Victoria had always prided herself on being a dedicated mother. With two children and a busy household to manage, she ran a tight ship, ensuring everything was in its place and every moment was accounted for. Her children's schedules were meticulously planned, their activities carefully curated, and their academic progress closely monitored. She believed this was the path to success and happiness for her kids.

However, as time went on, Victoria began to notice a growing distance between herself and her children. When they made mistakes or ran late for school, she found herself reacting with frustration and disappointment. The tension in their home was palpable, and Helen couldn't understand why her efforts to create the perfect environment weren't yielding the results she expected.

One day, during a particularly heated argument with her teenage daughter about a less-than-perfect test score, Victoria caught a glimpse of herself in the mirror. In that moment, she saw not just herself, but the shadow of her own mother—critical, demanding, and always pushing for perfection. The realization hit her like a ton of bricks: she had become the very thing she had vowed never to be.

This epiphany led Victoria on a journey of self-reflection. She began to reverse engineer her actions, finding that her frustration with her kids stemmed from a fear of not being a good enough mother and fear of her children's failures reflecting poorly on her. She realized how tightly controlling she had become, how every aspect of their lives had been confined to rigid frameworks in her quest for their success and safety.

As Victoria delved deeper into her motivations, she uncovered a part of herself that felt unfulfilled, a part that had unconsciously become a relentless cheerleader for her children's achievements. She had been living vicariously through them, pushing them to accomplish the dreams she had never pursued for herself.

With this newfound understanding, Victoria made a conscious decision to change. She began to loosen her grip on control and develop a genuine curiosity about her children as individuals. She realized that in her desire to check off all the boxes of good parenting, she had lost sight of the joy and spontaneity that should come with raising children.

Victoria started to create space for play and genuine connection. Instead of drilling her kids on homework, she'd ask about their interests and dreams. She learned to pause before reacting to perceived failures, choosing instead to respond with empathy and understanding. It wasn't always easy—old habits die hard—but Victoria was determined to rebuild the bridges she had unwittingly damaged.

Over time, Victoria's relationship with her children transformed. The house filled with more laughter and fewer arguments. Her children began to open up to her, sharing their thoughts and feelings more freely. Helen discovered that by letting go of her rigid expectations and embracing her children for who they were, she not only became a better mother but also found a sense of peace, joy, and fulfillment she had been missing all along.

PHASE 2 REFLECTIONS

In this second phase, you have two goals to accomplish:

The first one is to observe your Conditioned Self in action to gather information about your hidden desires, repressed fears, and the original trigger event.

The second one is to be alert every time you get triggered to catch the thoughts that ignite your emotions. Then simply reverse engineer those thoughts through conducting an internal investigation. You do that by challenging your thoughts with "What If, So What" questions until you reach a meaningful or reasonable repressed fear that resonates with you. Then, try to recall an original event that potentially formed this repressed fear.

For the next seven days, make a journal entry at the end of each day and write down your answers to the following questions:

1. How many times were you able to pause and observe your Conditioned Self in action during the day?

2. What thoughts, beliefs, values did you observe in your conditioned behavior?

3. Which hidden desires and repressed fears have you identified behind your Conditioned Self?

4. How did your conversations go with your parents, relatives, and friends about your past?

5. Which original trigger events did you recall that shed light on the Conditioned Self that you are today?

PHASE 3

EXPANDING YOUR BOUNDARIES

Once you connect the dots between the masks you wear and your past experiences, you'll understand the intricacies of how your subconscious programming intrinsically controls your life. The more you observe your Conditioned Self, the more you'll notice the contracted bounds of your comfort zone.

How can you become your Real Self, the best version of yourself, by playing it safe? You already know what happens when you make your life decisions out of fear: an unfulfilling, monotonous, stagnant life. This third phase you're about to enter encourages you to challenge your Conditioned Self by overriding its automatic, conditioned behavior.

You are about to get some fresh air beyond the tight borders of your comfort zone. But before you start expanding your contracted boundaries through conscious actions against your mask, let's establish why living in safety brings such a lower quality of life. Through the first two phases, you realized most of your time is spent either emotionally reacting to triggers (because they threaten your repressed fears) or acting your persona according to your hidden desires (to hide your repressed fears). Both actions are defensive and therefore make you exert your valuable personal energy, leading you to exhaustion and confusion.

You can imagine how this low mental and emotional state makes you withdraw from life and pushes you even further into your comfort zone. You don't want to go out. You don't want to explore new things. You have no curiosity about anything. You don't have time nor the energy to be creative. And most importantly, you don't want to expose yourself to these people who constantly trigger you. As you withdraw more, life becomes smaller and more contracted. You get more defensive. You double down on your masks. Over time, life turns into an unfulfilling experience.

OVERRIDING CONDITIONED BEHAVIORS

Most of us find ourselves in that contracted life without knowing how to get out. The main reason for not finding the path out of the comfort zone is fear. We built the comfort zone because it felt safe and secure. Why on earth would we leave, even though it's a tightly contracted space where we feel trapped and suffocated? At the same time, without such courage, the personal transformation, which takes place outside of your comfort zone, is not possible.

The conundrum of whether to stay with the status quo or to leave the safe life you've built can only be resolved by taking a small step at a time to experience an inch of the freedom available outside of your comfort zone. Only small but deliberate actions can free you from what's holding you back. Like a prisoner who uses his spare spoon to shovel dirt to dig a long tunnel out of his cell, you identify one conditioned behavior at a time and try to override it, one by one, step by step.

This arduous process of peeling away your mask pays off at the end when you bask your purified free spirit in the waters of self-realization. After all, the comfort zone you create, which is the matrix we all live in, can only be decoded by becoming aware of and understanding the opposing Selves, the Conditioned and Vulnerable brothers that cause the internal conflict that ruins our lives. Only when you catch yourself wearing one of your masks can you take action to chip away one little part of the protective shield. However, most of us can't fathom such courage of stepping out into the unknown and therefore feel deeply lost, confused, and paralyzed in almost every major life decision we make.

I suggest we look at these opposing forces in pairs to understand what kind of personas we often find ourselves oscillating in between. Keep in mind that the powerful, active force of your hidden desires shows up as your Conditioned Self, while the softer, inactive, passive force of your repressed fears manifests as your Vulnerable Self.

Let's dive in.

The force of the hidden desire to be perfect against the force of the repressed fear of not being good enough manifest as:

a. Perfectionist (Conditioned Self)

b. Procrastinator (Vulnerable Self)

The force of the hidden desire to be recognized versus the force of the repressed fear of not being recognized manifest as:

a. High Achiever (Conditioned Self)

b. Loser, Failure (Vulnerable Self)

The force of the hidden desire to be seen versus the force of the repressed fear of being dismissed manifest as:

a. Attention Seeker (Conditioned Self)

b. Loner, Independent (Vulnerable Self)

The force of the hidden desire to be valued versus the force of the repressed fear of not being appreciated manifest as:

a. People Pleaser (Conditioned Self)

b. Individualist, Withdrawn (Vulnerable Self)

The force of the hidden desire to be social and connected versus the force of the repressed fear of being abandoned or betrayed manifest as:

a. Social Butterfly (Conditioned Self)

b. Reserved, Isolated (Vulnerable Self)

Now you know why the world is in chaos. We all constantly live under these opposing personas without knowing who we really are. Our internal conflicts are reflected onto the outside world. No wonder nobody is happy. We all feel stuck in between these conditioned behaviors. We waste our precious energies defending our vulnerability and pretending that we are not "insecure." The personal freedom, which is your fuel on your path to self-realization, comes from breaking this vicious pendulum swing from one polarity to another.

Of course, going against your Conditioned Self is not an easy task, considering how many years of subconscious programming have governed your actions. Then, how is it even possible to override your conditioned behavior? This is where the third transformation strategy comes into play.

3RD TRANSFORMATION STRATEGY: DOING THE OPPOSITE

The Doing the Opposite strategy invites you to simply notice conditioned behaviors, whether they show up as the Conditioned Self or as the Vulnerable Self, and push back on them by doing something different. By changing things up, you challenge your repressed fears and expose your hidden desires.

Have you ever seen a tightrope walker perform? When you watch him walk, it may look like he is in perfect balance. Yet a closer look reveals that he's constantly adjusting where his weight lands. He's wobbly. His body goes to the right and then to the left, based on how the rope beneath him swings. How does he adjust his weight and find balance? He counteracts the weight that pulls him off balance.

In the Doing the Opposite strategy, you will do the same thing. The Doing the Opposite strategy helps you accomplish this task by balancing each force through constant counter adjustments against the conditioned behavior that will naturally make you face your vulnerability and chip away your fears until you find your natural center.

The only question is whether you could be conscious enough in the moment to challenge your mask and adjust your actions. When you observe your Vulnerable Self, can you counteract it by taking conscious actions to be more like your Conditioned Self? And vice versa?

You can appreciate how difficult it is to achieve such a high degree of awareness. As we talked about in Phase 1, you definitely need to establish an objective observer who is outside of yourself. Only in that state can you, as the observer of your own conditioned persona, consciously watch your Vulnerable and Conditioned Selves from a distance in an unattached way.

That cultivated distance or mental space gives you the power and agency to not get hooked into your conditioned reactions and actions. When you keep yourself separate from your programming, that's exactly the moment you can override your subconscious influences and counteract the masks you wear in any given moment.

Here are some specific examples of Doing the Opposite strategies:

- When you're acting like a perfectionist, make deliberate mistakes or consciously don't work as hard.

- When you're procrastinating, try to focus on the task at hand and get one part done in one sitting.

- When you find yourself working hard as a high achiever, slow down your efforts and do a few things without expecting to get anything out of it.

- When you feel like a failure, try to switch your energy and work on a project where you can achieve something and receive acknowledgment for that.

- When your conditioned behavior is to try to be accepted by certain people, try to act aloof, nonchalant, and unattached.

- When you wall yourself off because you fear being dismissed, lean in to conversations more and try to connect with people to get acceptance.

- When you act in ways that please others to receive their appreciation and acceptance, try to take more actions that honor your own values.

- When you feel uninterested in doing anything for others because you're fed up with giving them all your energy and time and receiving nothing in return, try offering a few favors to others.

These opposing masks are constantly battling with each other, and the internal conflict creates uneasiness, anxiety, and confusion in you. By consciously adjusting your actions to counteract your usual tendencies, you'll eventually achieve a state of balance and inner calm. This fosters a stronger sense of presence, which facilitates change that brings more joy and fulfillment to your life.

3RD TRANSFORMATION TECHNIQUE: PLAYING THE NUMBERS GAME

When you're caught in between these two conditioned personas, which have pretty much governed your entire life and created stagnancy, monotony, and lack of joy and fulfillment, you end up feeling out of balance.

When you are in that wobbly state, you naturally choose just to survive, get through the day instead of trying to thrive or make something out of your life. Your energy levels are low. Your motivation lacks. Your morale tanks, constantly in the gutter. Life gets dark and uncertain. Your boundaries tighten. You become too scared to explore life to its fullest potential. You sacrifice your life's potential to mediocrity and mundane.

However, just hang tight—things are about to change!

You can break free from this joyless, unfulfilled life by playing the Numbers Game. To play it, you'll estimate how much of your life you spend living according to each of your masks and calculate a corresponding percentage. Then, you'll try to bring their numbers closer to each other by using the Doing the Opposite strategy.

Let's do it. Take a step back from your busy life and observe yourself. In your daily interactions, what overall percentage of time would you assign to your Vulnerable Self, who is acting under the influence of your repressed fears, and what percentage would you give to your Conditioned Self, who is driven by your hidden desires?

Here's how you play the Numbers Game.

Let's say you wear a mask of a conflict avoider as your Conditioned Self. Your hidden desire is to avoid conflicts at all costs, and your repressed fear is being emotionally hurt by conflicts, which make you feel put down, dismissed, and pushed out. Of course, you can't control life, and you eventually find yourself in conflicts. However, 90 percent of the time, you play the role of a conformist so you can abort the confrontational situation. You simply don't want to get hurt, so you don't say anything. You walk away. You don't respond. Your Conditioned Self, the conflict avoider, is in full force.

On the other hand, what is your Vulnerable Self doing? It's hiding behind the conformist. However, you can't hide it forever, so about 10 percent of the time, it acts like the antagonist Conditioned Self and tries to create conflicts. You then become that person who goes against the authority, because you're fed up saying "yes, ma'am" or "yes, sir." As a result, you find yourself swinging between these two personalities, one extremely quiet and reserved and the other engaged in conflicts.

How do you equalize these percentages, in other words, bring them closer to each other, by playing the Numbers Game? Can you decrease your Conditioned Self to 85 percent by intentionally speaking up more and sharing your thoughts freely with others, remaining with conflict when it arises rather than walking away? This will naturally increase the Vulnerable Self to 15 percent, inching closer to equalization of your opposing personas. The primary challenge here is to be able to stay in the conflict and expose your Vulnerable Self to your repressed fears.

The process of equalizing the opposing forces of your Conditioned Self and Vulnerable Self is a scary proposition. Your subconscious has worked hard to keep you in your contracted comfort zone, and now you're getting ready to fly away. Tune in to how you feel as you intentionally loosen the subconscious grip on your conditioned actions, behavior patterns, and personality traits. You may feel disoriented. However, playing the Numbers Game is a necessary process of personal transformation. By challenging your conditioned nature, you allow your true nature to show up.

During your interactions over the course of your day, notice which mask you're wearing and do the opposite of what you normally would. Your goal is to bring the balance of your Conditioned Self and Vulnerable Self closer to 50:50. When you reach that point, the doors of your comfort zone simply open for you to take more conscious steps toward becoming more real and authentic.

Shall we explore some examples together to better understand how the Doing the Opposite strategy works and how the Numbers Game equalizes the battlefield between the opposing masks you constantly wear? Here we go.

Example 1

Charles battles with a fear of not being good enough. His Conditioned Self is a perfectionist and shows up about 75 percent of the time. He works hard to avoid being seen as disorganized, improper, or like he has a lack of discipline and integrity. Instead of enjoying the simple things, he turns everything he does into a task. It's all about how proper everything looks, how well it's done, and how efficient he is.

To override his Conditioned Self, Charles allows himself to make a mistake—just once—to see what happens. Of course, he faces the discomfort of letting others see he's not perfect. On another occasion when he has a lot of work to do, he decides to go to bed early instead of staying up past midnight to finish a project. He meditates, facing his discomfort, but sleeps well that night. Having slept more hours than usual, Charles feels refreshed in the morning; he finds himself more energized to work on his project and finishes it on time. As the results are intriguing and encouraging, he decides to continue playing the Numbers Game and starts to feel a sense of personal freedom as he chips away his perfectionist mask.

As we identified earlier, the opposite persona of the perfectionist mask is the mask of a procrastinator, which Charles wears about 25 percent of the time. He is constantly exhausted because all his energy goes into doing things properly. He tries to utilize every minute of his day for productive activities, and he feel sluggish the rest of the time. He lacks spontaneity, and therefore, he finds himself procrastinating when it comes to his personal activities that are fun.

Now, in those moments where he's exhausted, Charles pushes himself to be spontaneous and do some fun things without expecting something in return. From time to time, when he feels the heaviness of the perfectionism return, he inspires himself and gets motivated to do something fun, creative, or unstructured instead. He allows himself to feel the discomfort of not knowing what he's doing and tunes in to how it feels to let go of the perfectionist.

Example 2

Marnie has a fear of not being recognized. She (or rather, her Vulnerable Self) feels like a failure and a loser about 70 percent of the time. She doesn't have much energy or enthusiasm because she knows deep down, no matter how much she works, that she's not going to achieve anything or be successful. She has repeatedly experienced situations where others simply don't recognize her efforts. So why bother? As a result, Marnie always gives her minimum effort because it's not worth it.

When doing the opposite, Marnie's challenge is figuring out how to motivate this Vulnerable Self and do things to be recognized. This requires her to consciously push back against her "I'm a failure" attitude and trust that she can contribute in a meaningful way to a project that has some visibility and requires feedback from others. Marnie must get the guts to invest her time and energy to commit to accomplishing a task, small or big, with curiosity to see what kind of recognition she'll receive as a result of her efforts.

When her Vulnerable Self isn't in charge, Marnie's Conditioned Self, the high achiever, takes over about 30 percent of the time. During those times, she has plenty of energy and enthusiasm to work on things that will bring her success. But because it's only 30 percent of the time, her small achievements don't give her the fulfillment of achieving something big. In this case, doing the opposite will require increasing the amount of effort and work she puts into a project, or choosing a project with higher visibility that challenges her fear of not being recognized. Marnie's goal is to see how much focus and effort she can put into a higher stakes project until she gets the recognition she deserves.

Example 3

Shane struggles with the fear of being dismissed and not being appreciated. His Conditioned Self turns out to be a people pleaser and takes over about 80 percent of the time. He's eager to be accepted, valued, and appreciated by the people who are important to him. To meet his goals, Shane's constantly doing things "in service" to them, accommodating their needs and giving them more priority than he gives himself. He feels responsible for making other people happy and cheering them on, with the hope that he'll become irreplaceable, accepted, and included by the people whose love he needs so desperately.

The challenge here is for Shane to pull back his people pleaser side so that he starts to feel some doubt and discomfort around how these people are going to interact with him. To that extent, whenever he senses that he's doing something and expecting acknowledgment and appreciation for it, he'll stop doing whatever he's doing and see what happens. At the very least, he tries to dampen his enthusiasm for connecting with those people and lets his relationships with them flow more naturally. He doesn't have to volunteer on every occasion to prove that he's an irreplaceable resource.

On the other side, Shane's Vulnerable Self, who gives in to his repressed fears, feels dismissed and not appreciated about 20 percent of the time. During those times, he reacts emotionally to not getting what he wants for his efforts. As a result, he checks out and hides behind emotional walls, feeling dismissed and unappreciated. He slowly and intentionally distances himself from the people whose approval he used to crave.

When he experiences this disappointment, instead of becoming detached, nonchalant, and uninterested in doing anything because he's fed up with not receiving appreciation, Shane does something to meet their expectations. Instead of intentionally creating an emotional gap between himself and the people he used to try to please, he turns around and gets a little bit closer to them. His Doing the Opposite response is to ask them if they need help, without immediately offering it. He must loosen up a little and melt the ice between himself and others in contentious moments and turn his isolation into a bridge to reach out to connect with them again.

How can you apply some of these strategies in your daily life? Consider how you can extend these examples to apply to all the different masks you wear in your interactions with others throughout your day.

Real Life Scenario

Henry is a penny-pincher, coupon collector, and sandwich card holder. He constantly complains about how much time he wastes watching TV or scrolling so many social media feeds. He has no idea that he's trying to escape from his unfulfilling life and doing all of that in the name of numbing an overly restricted life without any excitement and meaningful experiences.

How can he live his life when he's so focused on money? He limits his travel. He doesn't go out much. He gets a special kick out of collecting stamps on his sandwich card. He drives his wife crazy, by saving coupons and buying things at discount.

Henry is a hard worker. He takes his job seriously. He earns a decent salary, yet it causes him so much stress as he doesn't want to be fired. Therefore, he works more than anybody. He jumps on every project to prove his worth to his boss and top management. When he comes home, he feels exhausted. He prefers not to talk much. After dinner, he sits on the couch and watches TV to numb his unhappiness and to keep himself occupied along with occasional internet surfing and social media feeds. He's okay with all of that and sees it as cheap entertainment as he lives vicariously through others' experiences.

Deep down, he yearns for a different life but can't figure out how to get there. If he's honest with himself, he has all the desires of going out, tasting the menus of expensive restaurants, traveling to exotic places, staying in five-star hotels, driving luxury sports cars, wearing designer watches. He embarks on his transformation journey and becomes aware that his penny-pinching Conditioned Self is constraining his life.

One night, Henry finds himself driving downtown to meet his wife in the city. She's staying overnight in a hotel for a business conference, and he was going to stay with her. They made dinner plans to enjoy the city together. When he pulls into the hotel entrance, he decides to use the valet, as part of his Doing the Opposite strategy, just to push back against his penny-pincher mask. However, when he learns that valet parking costs seventy dollars a night, he immediately abandons the idea and drives off to look for a parking spot on the streets of downtown.

He starts to circle around the city without any luck finding a parking spot. Feeling frustrated, he decides to pay the valet and be done with his misery. After all, he feels content as he's forced to do the opposite. Thus, he welcomes the idea to get out of his comfort zone and pay for the valet. However, as he turns around the corner on his way back to the hotel, he sees a spot about twenty yards away from the hotel entrance. It's a miracle, he thinks! Without any hesitation, he rushes over and parks before anyone can take the empty spot.

The next morning, he wakes up early as he needs to hit the road to avoid the morning traffic before the city streets get jammed. He gets ready for the day and has his free breakfast in the hotel, included in the room rate paid by his wife's company. Then, full and happy, he walks out of the hotel toward his car.

As he gets closer to his car, he suddenly notices something stuck on the windshield wiper. He squints his eyes to better see what it is. He sees a white envelope flipping in the morning wind. He yells, "Wait a minute! What is that?!" As he takes the envelope in his hands, he can't believe his eyes.

As he opens the envelope, his hands shaking uncontrollably, he confirms his suspicion that it is a parking ticket. Apparently, when he parked the night before, and as he rushed off to meet his wife for dinner, which he was unfashionably late for, he failed to pay attention to the sign, which read: No Parking: Street Cleaning Tuesday at 5 a.m. That's probably why nobody parked there on Monday night. As he put on his reading glasses to check the financial damage of his mistake, he couldn't help but laugh out loud, as the ticket cost him exactly what he could've paid to the valet about thirty yards away: seventy dollars!

For the rest of the day, Henry has only one thing on his mind: to override his conditioned penny-pincher once and for all. He determines that he's no longer obedient to his ego, to the Conditioned Self that constantly whispers to him to save more money. He pulls up all of his sandwich cards out of his thick, messy wallet and starts to cut them in pieces. He throws the coupons for the local grocery store into the recycle bin in the office and says goodbye to all "buy one, get one free" offers for the rest of his life.

The following week, Henry starts to put his actions where his mind has been. He starts doing the opposite by making reservations to a few high-end, high-quality restaurants (but not a Michelin star yet), where he decides not to look at the prices while picking the meals. He then books a hot air balloon ride with champagne for his wife's birthday. He intentionally starts spending money on good quality experiences without making a fuss or calculating its costs. A few months later, Henry and his wife are seen at the local popular jazz club. Henry's life has never looked the same ever again, as he constantly chooses to expand the borders of his comfort zone, which grows exponentially as he has freed himself of his Conditioned Self and become more real with every step he takes.

PHASE 3 REFLECTIONS

From here on, try to take as many direct and conscious actions as possible to challenge your masks. You want to create a stronger presence as an objective outside observer of your masks. If you can do that, you'll have an easier time pausing and observing your masks, applying the Doing the Opposite strategy and joyfully playing the Numbers Game to bring your opposing masks to an equilibrium.

For the next seven days, make a journal entry at the end of each day and write down your answers to the following questions:

1. What were your top three repressed fears and what percentage of your actions felt like your Conditioned Self and your Vulnerable Self?

2. How many times did you remember to pause and observe the masks you were wearing during the day?

3. When did you play the Numbers Game and apply the Doing the Opposite strategy? How did you feel getting out of your comfort zone?

4. What kind of actions did you take to challenge your Conditioned Self and pull back on your hidden desires? How did it feel not doing your conditioned behavior?

5. What actions did you take where you did not give in to your Vulnerable Self and you faced your repressed fears?

PHASE 4

BRINGING PEACE TO YOUR INNER CONFLICT

In Phase 4, you are going to finish what you started in Phase 3, continuing to practice the Doing the Opposite strategy until your actions are completely balanced at 50:50 between your Conditioned Self and your Vulnerable Self. When the opposing forces of repressed fears and hidden desires equalize, the intensity of the internal conflict that causes you mental and emotional suffering dissipates.

At that point, the gravity of both sides of your personas melts away, and you feel neutral and centered. You embrace objectivity and nonattachment. That tranquil space naturally gives birth to your Conscious Self.

Without realizing, you've already been working on developing this Conscious Self. It's the independent witness. It's the objective observer. In utilizing the Numbers Game, slowly but surely, you've been giving your Conscious Self more and more presence. Every time you pause and observe your Conditioned Self or Vulnerable Self, your Conscious Self gains its presence and claims its power. Whenever you embody your Conscious Self, you can then take more conscious control over your actions, reducing the governance of your subconscious over your conditioned personas.

Think of this newly emerging Self as the bridge between your subconscious personalities (your current masks) and your Real Self (your de-conditioned true essence). The Conscious Self is the one who's above your two polarized conditioned forces. Therefore, once you integrate them and melt them into each other, the resulting presence is part of you that becomes deeply aware of what's really going on in any given situation. That freshly awakening Conscious Self is more alert than ever in each present moment and can wisely discern what conscious actions you need to take to create that special mental, emotional, and physical space for your Real Self to emerge.

REINFORCING YOUR RESISTANCE

In the beginning, it'd be foolish to expect to embody your Conscious Self 24/7. However, try to notice how you move in and out of that state throughout the day. Of course, fostering that kind of presence is in your hands. The more often you use the Doing the Opposite strategy, the more conscious your actions become. With the aim of balancing the opposing forces at 50:50, you keep playing the Numbers Game to have a better chance for your Conscious Self to show up in your life.

Now, how can you most successfully integrate your opposing Selves?

By reinforcing your resistance and strengthening your stance against your conditioned behaviors, which is basically a continued effort in the Doing the Opposite strategy.

Whenever you manage to inhabit your Conscious Self (and it's an inner feeling more than a mental realization), try to notice what kind of influence you are under at that moment. When you become the independent observer of yourself, sense the charge in your body, decipher whether it's coming from your hidden desires and repressed fears. Then, empower your Conscious Self to go against your conditioned actions and override your character traits, behavior patterns, and ingrained personas to expose your vulnerability and insecurity.

From this perspective, embracing the two opposing forces that show up as your personas is a form of resistance against your subconscious. The Doing the Opposite strategy supports such resistance, when you no longer give in to the demands of certain conditioned behaviors. When you're able to override them, you declare disobedience to your subconscious.

This presence is what allows your Conscious Self to become more in charge of your life. Since the beginning of your journey, you've been trying to build this Conscious Self who is simply the one who pauses and observes the tangible force that influences your conditioned behaviors. When you become more of your Conscious Self, you start to feel this force more intimately in your body, in the way of physical sensations.

This tight connection with the charge that each opposing force creates in your body is an important component of integration. To successfully execute such complex strategy, you want to develop the ability to stay with the uncomfortable physical sensations. When you consciously sit in that discomfort, you naturally increase your resistance against your Conditioned Self and Vulnerable Self.

4TH TRANSFORMATION STRATEGY: STAYING WITH CONSCIOUS DISCOMFORT

Like the emotional charge you feel in the body, which is mainly a force of your Vulnerable Self—anger, anxiety, frustration, and sadness—you can also sense a force that your subconscious creates as a sensation in your body to create the persona, the Conditioned Self.

For example, when you're playing the role of a perfectionist with hidden desires of being good and perfect, you have a charge in your body that your subconscious creates to make you act like a perfectionist. The opposite is also true. When you're acting like a procrastinator who gives in to your repressed fears of not being good enough, you notice a different charge: a heaviness, sluggishness, or stagnancy in your body that prevents you from acting inspired and motivated.

You need to drop into your body to connect with the physical sensations that these subconscious forces create. Once you locate them, you basically access the part of the body where your first emotional wound, feeling, or repressed fear was stored by your subconscious during the original trigger event. When you acknowledge this heavy force that shows up as discomfort, you connect with its physical sensations and immediately sense your vulnerabilities and insecurities.

Acknowledging such emotional pain and consciously sitting with the discomfort from this integration perspective is not an easy action to take. However, since you've been running away from discomfort, you can imagine how turning around and facing your emotional pain could yield amazing transformation.

When you apply the Conscious Discomfort strategy, you transform yourself from the victim of the past to victor of the future. By staying with the physical sensations of the subtle yet strong forces of your subconscious, you bring out what's been suppressed and give yourself a chance to process what happened in the past. Due to its intensity, this technique requires deeper awareness and thorough understanding of your masks before being implemented in the Integration strategy.

As you sit with these painful sensations more and more and welcome them to practice Conscious Discomfort, you start getting ready for the Integration strategy. You want to be very familiar with where these charges are located so that you can integrate them physically within your body. The Integration strategy is a somatic practice. It takes place in the body.

4TH TRANSFORMATION TECHNIQUE: INTEGRATING OPPOSING PERSONAS

Let's go through the steps of how to integrate and neutralize your opposing forces for a stronger presence in your life. The Integration strategy is pivotal to help you transition from the automatic action of the subconscious to the discernment of the higher consciousness. In a sense, it's the alchemy of two opposing forces that ultimately creates the Conscious Self.

How do you create such powerful alchemy? Below is a quick step-by-step guide on how to integrate your opposing masks and bring your personas together. Try to read through it first, and then, before moving on to the example, try to apply each step to your unique situation. Once you fully experience these steps, you may sense a positive shift in your consciousness.

1. Find a comfortable place to sit. Place your feet flat on the floor. Let your hands rest on your lap, palms facing down.

2. Select a recent trigger event that you experienced during an intense emotional reaction.

3. Close your eyes. Bring up the situation in your mind. Start looking at this trigger event like an objective outside observer, yet also relive it at the same time.

4. Pause to notice your emotional reaction.

5. Observe your Vulnerable Self and its thoughts and feelings about the person or situation that created the trigger.

6. Drop in your body and sense the emotional charge as a physical sensation. Where do you feel it? Connect with it, and pick it up with your right hand as if you're picking up an apple from a tree. Then, simply imagine holding its energy in your right palm. To capture it, make a fist and place it facing down on your right knee.

7. Name the charge that you're holding in your right fist. How would you describe this repressed fear that your Vulnerable Self feels as a result of the trigger event? What kind of statements would describe this feeling? Feel free to use any word or phrase or short sentence to describe how this energy resonates within you.

8. After you tune in to your right fist and connect with the name of the energy, come up with the opposite name— its opposite energy. For example, if you named the right fist energy "loser," then connect with the energy of a "winner."

9. With your eyes closed, recall a memory where you felt this opposing energy. (In this example, the charge of the "winner" energy.) Pause and observe your Conditioned Self, as a "winner" in that situation. Then, drop into your body and feel the physical sensations you felt in your body at the time. This is where the force of your hidden desires, the Conditioned Self, shows up as a charge in the body.

10. Tune in to the charge of the "winner" in your body and pick it up with your left palm, again, as if you're picking up an apple from a tree, and make a fist to capture its energy. Place it on your left knee, fist facing down.

11. In the last step of the Integration strategy, tighten both fists. Take a deep breath into the center of your chest while holding your focus on both of your tight fists simultaneously. Exhale, imagining the charges that you hold in both fists are being released into the air out of your mouth. Do this three times in total.

12. No matter where the energies of your opposing personas show up in your body, always use chest as an integration center. After the third exhale, and release of all the conditioned energies of your personas out of your mouth, bring your focus back to the center of your chest to neutralize your energies. Open your eyes.

It's hard to describe the mental, emotional, and physical state you find yourself in after integration. It's a place or space where you feel that you're on your own, standing on your feet, in your power, without any fears and any desires. You sense utmost peace and neutral detachment from everything around you. In some cases, either during integration or the days after integration, you have clarity on what actions to take in any particular moment to open yourself up to your true essence, to your authentic self-expression, and ultimately, become your Real Self.

Therefore, every time you complete this Integration strategy, you may experience a sense of deep calmness within your body, as well as in your mind. Some of my clients feel a soft movement of energy or tingling as physical sensations in different parts of their body. You experience this positive shift in your mental, emotional, and physical energy because you neutralize the static electricity or uncomfortable charge that the two opposing forces of your Conditioned Self and Vulnerable Self create in your body.

When you release this charge through the Integration strategy, you feel empowered to turn the chaos to peace and uncertainty to clarity with more centered and grounded presence. Through this awakened sense of inner power, you can now override your conditioned behaviors much easier and more comfortably without any guilt, fear, or shame associated with your "Doing the Opposite" actions.

We can also explain this phenomenon with an energy scale analogy. Imagine there exists a measurement device that can read your energy level, the frequency or vibration of the electromagnetic field of your body. It's a scale of 1 to 100. With the tug-of-war happening between your Conditioned Self and Vulnerable Self, your energy level is, let's say, around fifteen. It's low because the static energy these two opposing forces create pulls your energy down.

Now, when you integrate them—in a way, digest them—within your body, you basically release the negative energy that your body has carried due to this internal conflict you've been exposed to your entire life. Then what happens? Your energy level naturally expands and increases, let's say, to twenty-five. This energetic jump brings a deeper calmness and a sense of centeredness and groundedness that you may be feeling after the Integration strategy but have rarely felt in your life before.

One more note on the energy levels. When I say high-energy levels, I'm not referring to being "hyper." In our society, we see social butterflies, influencers, and motivational speakers as high-energy beings and admire them for their relentless active state. However, they're actually under the influence of their high achiever Conditioned Self, who needs to exude high energy to attract attention.

That's a very exhausting activity for them, and they need to take breaks to replenish their energy levels to be back in front of the public. If they could integrate their repressed fears and hidden desires, they could be more impactful and influential with calmer and more powerful energy that is high in frequency and less static, which may result in attracting fewer people than before, but will maintain better health in the process and possibly have a deeper impact on the world.

REAL LIFE SCENARIO

For years, Kathy had been the quintessential people pleaser, constantly putting the needs and expectations of others before her own. She would anticipate what those around her wanted, scrambling to meet their demands and ensure they were happy. But no matter how much she gave, it never seemed to be enough.

Whenever Kathy's efforts were met with rejection, disagreement, or indifference, she would find herself feeling deeply hurt and unappreciated. The anger and disappointment would well up inside her, and she would retreat, isolating herself and erecting walls of distrust. Her constant desire to be needed and validated had become a heavy burden, weighing her down and preventing her from truly living.

Then one day, Kathy decided it was time for a change. She began to recognize the patterns of her people-pleasing tendencies and how they were negatively impacting her own well-being. Slowly, she started doing the opposite to discern the behavior of her Conditioned Self, the people pleaser, from the Vulnerable Self, who would react and retreat. As a result, she was able to integrate both parts of herself more effectively, choosing to respond with more neutrality when the urge to help others overtook her.

Rather than assuming she knew what others needed, Kathy started to ask questions, allowing them to express their own desires. This simple shift gave her a newfound sense of ease, no longer feeling the need to shoulder the responsibility of catering to everyone else's needs.

As Kathy's attention began to turn inward, she realized something profound: she had never truly paid attention to her own wants and needs. For so long, it had been all about others, leaving little room for her to explore her own interests and passions. She didn't even know what she wanted for herself.

Kathy decided to change that. On weekends, she began to venture out, discovering hidden gems in her own town that she had never noticed before. Neighborhoods she had passed by countless times were suddenly alive with fascinating historical sites, cozy cafés, and charming old buildings. It was as if she was seeing the world through new eyes, like a newborn taking in the wonders of their surroundings.

This newfound sense of freedom and discovery filled Kathy with excitement. No longer confined by the need to please others, she could finally breathe and focus on her own desires. She started planning domestic trips, eager to explore other cities and quench her thirst for adventure.

And as Kathy's need for self-exploration grew, her urge to people-please began to subside. As a result, she found herself no longer retreating or putting up walls when her need for appreciation was not met. She no longer felt the urge to deplete her energy or suppress her own feelings to make others happy. Instead, she found a newfound balance, able to offer help and support when it felt genuine, without the burden of others' expectations of her.

PHASE 4 REFLECTIONS

The goal of this phase is to continue the Doing the Opposite strategy until you bring the percentages of your Conditioned Self and Vulnerable Self to a perfect balance of 50:50. When you reach that equilibrium, you give your Conscious Self space to emerge. You feel a sense of neutrality, a sense of detachment when you observe your conditioned actions. You are free of self-judgment or labels of others when your Conscious Self is in charge of your conscious actions. Its rise to power comes from being more and more present in the now. This strong presence allows you to apply your new technique, the integration of your masks.

To execute this technique successfully, you need to drop into your body and sense the physical sensations of the opposing conditioned forces. Through this connection to your body you integrate your masks fully as they melt into each other. The Conscious Discomfort strategy helps you stay with these forces without giving in to them, which creates a natural discomfort as you get out of your conditioned actions. As you practice staying with the physical sensations, you'll slowly develop essential skills for expanding your boundaries, which builds a stronger foundation for a new life with more joy and fulfillment.

For the next seven days, make a journal entry at the end of each day and write down your answers to the following questions:

1. When reflecting on your conditioned actions today, what percentage of time would you give to your Conditioned Self and how much would you give to your Vulnerable Self?

2. What did you name the mask for your Conditioned Self and your Vulnerable Self?

3. How well did you drop into your body and feel the physical sensations or the charge of each force?

4. What did you feel when practicing Conscious Discomfort?

5. How did you feel before your Integration strategy, and how did you feel afterward?

PHASE 5

DISCOVERING WHAT'S IMPORTANT TO YOU

Once the opposing forces of your masks melt into each other on the battlefield of your inner world, your Conscious Self stands up, ready to take command of your life. With that heightened awareness and presence, you're happy to give authority to your Conscious Self to override your subconscious and allow it to steer your life with more purpose and integrity.

Therefore, in this phase, you change gears. Your transformation journey is no longer about fine-tuning your conditioned actions, but to bring more of your Conscious Self into your daily life. Doing this naturally awakens you to new possibilities for a future different from today, and hopefully brighter than ever. Certainly, you now understand very well that the more you make your true essence part of your life, the more joy and fulfillment you experience.

Why was this awakening not possible before? Because your Conscious Self has been dormant for your entire life. Your subconscious brokered a deal with you. It completely shut your Conscious Self down in exchange for your safety and comfort. Your subconscious didn't trust you to make the right decisions, so it stayed in power.

On the other hand, you didn't trust others, so you gave the reins of your life to your subconscious and succumbed to your comfort zone.

In a sense, you sacrificed your true essence to the repressed fears and hidden desires that governed your life and made it unfulfilling. Now that your Conscious Self is emerging with stronger presence and is enjoying its ability to take conscious actions in the now, you can easily see how every step you take can align you with your true essence and get you connected with the slowly appearing glimpses of your Real Self.

How do you know what your true essence is? How would you recognize if you caught a sliver of your Real Self? This phase offers the answers to these very important questions and becomes a gateway to your new life.

This is the phase where you go from your limited, contracted existence that comes from blindly or subconsciously following the values you borrowed from your parents, friends, environment, community, and society to discovering your own values that are important and meaningful to you. During this transition phase, you'll slowly start to drop the values that don't serve you anymore as you embrace the new ones that uplift you toward becoming your Real Self.

IDENTIFYING YOUR PERSONAL VALUES

The difficulty lies in identifying which values are real and represent your true essence. Let's face it. You already live according to your values. However, those values have been defined by your subconscious programming. You created concepts, thoughts, beliefs, mission statements, or opinions on life that seemed to be important and meaningful to you. How did you form them? Through the influence of your past experiences.

These values have motivated you and directed your actions throughout your life. Every action you take comes from your values, which affect your life decisions. The way you honor your values and the priority you give to each of them may have changed from time to time. However, you maintain the set of values that your Conditioned Self adopted to survive in the world.

Of course, your subconscious programming took charge and formed a set of values to hide your vulnerabilities and insecurities and reinforce the mask of your Conditioned Self. Life decisions made according to those values subconsciously made you contract your boundaries and pulled you into the limited, unfulfilling life you experience today.

Now, pause for a moment here. Do you even know what values you live by today? Are you aware of how many of the values you honor today are actually yours? How many of them have you borrowed from your parents, friends, community, environment, and society? Which of those values limit your life and make you stay in your comfort zone?

DISCOVERING YOUR OWN VALUES

Let's explore life at a deeper level and find out the answers to these questions together. Note that this quest is not a mental exercise but a practical life experiment. You simply identify your personal values and connect with them through trial and error through feeling. Such feeling is a feedback loop that you receive from your experiments with different options and discerning how each experience makes you feel inside afterward.

For example, when you gather with your friends over lunch and talk about this and that, what kind of feeling do you leave the meeting with? Compare that with the feeling of having a walk in the park with beautiful trees and a pond while listening to your favorite podcast. Do you sense the difference? I'm not saying one is better than the other. They strike different inner feelings that you want to be aware of so that you can make better, more conscious decisions in the future. You can choose different options according to what you need to nourish your soul in that moment.

As your Conscious Self takes over more of your daily decision-making processes, your personal values will start to naturally appear. Remember, your Conscious Self is the one who's aware and awake. When you do something that doesn't align with your true essence, you'll feel a sense of discomfort or disappointment. When you allow yourself to consciously explore life, be more and more present, and discern what you like and don't like about each experience, your personal values will start to take shape and become more evident to you.

And no rush, please! You have your entire life to discover your personal values. Once you open yourself up to new experiences, life will provide plenty of opportunities for you to test out your preferences and figure out what is and isn't important to you. In each and every moment, practice inward attention to feel the connection with your inner world, your desires, and your inner feelings. They will announce to you more and more clearly what particular experiences resonate with your true essence. Let your inner feelings, not your hidden desires, ignite your passion for life and connect you with a deeper sense of your true essence, guiding you toward your personal values.

When experimenting with different life experiences, having innocent, childlike curiosity is a huge advantage. Deep curiosity is the cure, the propeller that will push you out of your comfort zone inch by inch. Try not to shoot for the stars in the beginning, as your subconscious programming will be guarding the gates and may not allow you to stray too far from your ego values and Conditioned Self. Therefore, be prepared to take three steps forward and two steps back when discovering your personal values and implementing them into your life.

But even if this ends up being the case, keep curiously exploring life and patiently try new actions and new directions, building on the self-awareness you acquire from each experience. Every experiment can and will serve as a teaching moment for you to understand your true essence, as long as your Conscious Self is in charge and you're fully present while having these experiences.

WHAT'S MISSING IN YOUR LIFE?

To gain a deeper understanding of your personal values, it's also helpful to look at what's not working in your life. Highlighting what's not flowing or what you're not aligned with helps you discover what's missing in your life and leads you to discover new personal values that are more important to you than the ones you're honoring today.

Let's say you don't like your job. Before you started your Journey Within, your mind might have said, *I hate my job!* and your heart might have responded with a suggestion to take time off and go on vacation or simply quit and find a new job. Meanwhile, you'd have been confused about where to go or what to do. So instead of taking concrete action, your decision might have lingered for a while, causing you more stress and feelings of being trapped and stuck. As a result, you decide, *I'm just going to go out with some friends tonight, get drunk, and forget about everything.*

This might be a typical situation under the influence of your subconscious, with coping mechanisms in action and your Conditioned Self and Vulnerable Self pushing different agendas for you to follow. At this level of your journey, you might have a different set of actions. You may still hate your job, but now that you know how to do the opposite to override your conditioned actions, your coping mechanisms may be different. You may recognize how your job is misaligned with your personal values, and instead of being a victim of the situation, you might reevaluate and start taking actions toward honoring those particular values that are missing in your current job or look for jobs that honor those values that are important to you.

Changing your coping mechanisms, working on your addictions, and regulating your negative emotional reactions are signs of living with integrity. Achieving this kind of presence, with conviction that you have the power to change your life, deepens your reflections on your internal conflicts, complaints, and resentments, as well as on your inner feelings and self-knowledge, all helping you strongly pave the path toward your self-realization.

In such a state of awakening, every challenging situation you deal with appears to offer a variety of different options that you may not have been aware of before. In these mind expanding moments, you can't help but think whether these newly available opportunities existed before. But the reality is, you couldn't see them because your consciousness level wasn't as high as it is now.

In the above situation where you hate your job, there's another option available to you now. What if you decided to talk to your boss about how unfulfilled you feel in your current position and asked them whether more fulfilling opportunities are available within the company? Certainly, such action will challenge your mask, but wouldn't this option offer more hope for resolution versus going out with your friends to drink the night away and forget your unhappiness, showing up more disgruntled the next day?

Of course, after standing up for yourself and claiming your power (instead of being a victim to the situation), you may still feel that the possibility of getting transferred to a new role or to another department is futile. Then, of course, you may consider reaching out to recruiters to find another job that can fulfill your values.

Another option might be to list specific things that you are missing in your current role to identify what personal values you're not honoring. Maybe making that list inspires you to take steps to bring them into your life in a different way, such as through volunteering, working on creative projects, mentoring, or coaching at your kids' schools. In one way or another, honoring the personal values that are important to you will eventually lift the heavy weight you feel in your day-to-day grind and inject some energy into your life.

The bottom line is that when you allow your Conscious Self to step in and consciously look at problems, you are able to evaluate the root cause of your unhappiness from a different perspective and no longer see things in a black-and-white, either-or mode. At this level of self-awareness in this awakened state, your Conscious Self invites your Real Self to step in and identify the shades of gray that exist between the extreme options and help you see your preferences more clearly.

Here's a list of values that you can use to figure out what you would rather have in your life to feel that sense of joy and fulfillment.

- Acknowledgment
- Adventure
- Aesthetics
- Balance
- Beauty
- Being Known
- Calmness
- Collaboration
- Community
- Creativity
- Elegance
- Family
- Financial Freedom
- Free Spirit
- Harmony
- Honesty
- Humor
- Independence
- Integrity
- Joy
- Legacy
- Nature
- Orderliness
- Partnership
- Peace
- Personal Freedom
- Personal Growth
- Productivity
- Quality of Life
- Recognition
- Romance
- Safety
- Security
- Self-Care
- Self-Expression
- Self-Nurturing
- Service
- Socializing
- Solitude
- Spirituality
- Spontaneity
- Stability
- Success
- Taking Risks
- Tradition
- Travel
- Trust
- Vitality

Now review each value carefully. Circle the ones that could cure your complaints. Write them down. Reflect on them. Once you decide on a value, "test" it out.

Visualize it in your life. How does it feel? Can this value potentially bring more joy and fulfillment to you?

When doing this exercise, connect with your inner feelings for each personal value you identify and explore how it would feel when you honor them. Through this introspection, you basically reflect on what's missing in your life, and how you're about to fill that void.

After reviewing these values, which ones do you feel can bring joy, fulfillment, and meaning to your life? Which ones resonate with you the most and could cure your complaints? Please circle them.

INCORPORATING PERSONAL VALUES INTO LIFE

Now that you've started to connect with some personal values that are different from the ones you currently live by, how can you bring them to your life?

To accomplish this goal, you can incorporate these steps into your practice:

1. Identify your top five values that you picked from the list above.

2. Prioritize them according to their importance and how much you want to honor them in your life.

3. Write down what specific actions you would like to take so they become part of your daily life.

Note that you can work on just one value at a time or choose to work on several concurrently. For example, you can work on honoring "open communication" and incorporate it as a value into your relationship while also adding "helping others" as a career value, maybe by mentoring someone at work or signing up to volunteer at a nonprofit.

Be careful about not pushing or forcing yourself into a particular activity just to connect with a personal value. Instead, first observe what you're drawn to. Note that this connection is always mutual and interconnected. You feel drawn to it and the opportunity draws you in. Just observe what kind of opportunities you have in front of you. What *feels* the most joyful and fulfilling? When you have a conflict between your different values, look at your inner feelings and how the activity resonates within you. What is it you'd like to do? What *feels* like the right opportunity?

The distinction is often very subtle. Let's say one of your personal values is to help others. Instead of trying to enroll in a certification or graduate program to become a counselor or a therapist, connect with the feeling of *doing* it. What kind of opportunities do you have available to you right now to help others without investing a huge amount of time and money in relevant courses? Understand what attracts you about counseling as a career. Question how it's going to honor your personal values. Visualize how you will feel doing it day in, day out. As you go through these inner reflections and connect with deeper insights, in time, the right opportunity will come your way and reveal itself to you.

5TH TRANSFORMATION STRATEGY: GOING FROM COMPLAINTS TO VALUES

Another way to discover your personal values is to pay attention to your complaints. When you complain about a situation, that usually means the situation is not aligned with your true essence and that you're not honoring one of your personal values. If that's the case, ask yourself what you're complaining about and what's bothering you deep down.

You might consider summarizing the root of your complaint and asking this one simple inquisitive "why" question while doing your inquiry and introspection.

Why are you not happy with your relationship?

Why are you not happy with your current job?

Why are you not happy with your career?

When you ask these "why" questions with utmost neutral curiosity and without judgment or resentment, you invite yourself to reflect more deeply on your complaints, tuning in to what's missing in your life and what it is that you really want. What are you really complaining about? What needs are not getting fulfilled? What values are missing?

Without finger-pointing at others for their wrongdoings, bring your attention inward and understand *your* preferences. What matters to you? What's important in life? What makes your heart beat faster? What excites you? What brings you joy? What makes you feel fulfilled? What's meaningful to you? No matter what others think, answer these questions for yourself, not with your head but with your heart, and open yourself up to more experiments with life to find answers through the experiences you have.

Consider some of the following scenarios that may be applicable to your life situation. Let them inspire you to gain clarity and make better decisions when navigating challenges.

Scenario 1: Looking for the Right Person

Let's say you want to date and get into a long-term relationship. Why do you want to date? Do you want to find someone to share your life with, or do you just want someone to keep you company? What kind of person would you like to date? Why them in particular? What kind of chemistry would you like to have in your relationship with this person? Do you have any specific interests, ideas, feelings, or life goals that connect you more deeply with some people over others?

Scenario 2: Leaving a Long-term Relationship

Let's say you want to break up with your partner. Why do you want to leave this relationship? Do you deserve better? Why? What don't you like about this relationship? What is your ideal relationship? What kind of relationship will make you feel fulfilled, seen, and heard? What kind of person would you like to be with in your ideal relationship? How do your personal values match your relationship ideals?

Scenario 3: Seeking Promotion at Work

Let's say you're trying to get promoted. Why do you want that promotion? Do you want to make more money? Do you want to expand the size of your team, so you feel more self-worth and importance? Do you want to work on different projects and connect with new people to enhance your career? In other words, how does a promotion reflect your true essence?

Scenario 4: Choosing your Friends

Let's say you have different group of friends. Why do you choose to hang out with a particular set of friends more than the others? What happens when you see a certain friend? When you come home from a gathering, do you feel exhausted or energized? Do you jump on every opportunity with excitement to engage socially, or do you accept their invitation just to please everyone? Do you enjoy the conversations and activities, or would you prefer to do your own thing?

Scenario 5: Buying a New Car

You can even discover your personal values when you're buying a car. What kind of car are you considering? Why that car? Are you buying it because everyone says it's a great car, or because it gives you a certain aura, status, look, or appeal? How do you like the feeling of being in that car? In general, how does it feel to drive it? Which car connects with your inner passion? Which car, what design, and which brand truly reflects your true essence?

Using this style of questioning on every life decision, you acquire a new perspective that your Conscious Self uses to discern which actions can bring you joy and fulfillment and what actions don't. Therefore, all you have to do is to fully experience your values to curiously determine how they resonate with you internally.

When you bring such deep curiosity into your experiences and reflect on how your choices end up making you feel, you notice subtle internal cues that clarify your preferences and their importance to you. This clarity often invites you to make changes in your outer life that reflect how your true essence feels inside. Soon after, you start to experience a positive shift in your life that brings a profound sense of ease and flow that you haven't felt before.

FACING POSSIBLE OBSTACLES

Once you determine the actions you'd like to take to bring your personal values into your life, try not to turn these actions into long-term plans. You want to maintain your spontaneity and playfulness with more impromptu motivation for brief engagements that you make on a daily basis, rather than committing yourself to a goal for an extended period of time.

The reason for that is, setting goals may have a more deterring effect on your actions than being inspired and motivated. This is simply due to the fact that your mind and your body are not ready for a big change. When you come up with grand plans, when you set goals to accomplish in a set period of time, you put too much stress on the mind and the body. That stress creates pressure, and after a few days or a few weeks, you find yourself exhausted and ready to quit what you started a few days or weeks ago. In that low mental state, you may even forget why you're doing this and lose your connection with your values that once felt important to you.

Therefore, you want to be very careful and systematic about bringing your values slowly into your life. Maybe it's worth repeating with more emphasis here: your Real Self only emerges when your aware and awake Conscious Self starts taking actions to honor those personal values that are important and meaningful to you. When you are not fully integrated, your subconscious maintains its control over your actions, and as a result, internal conflict still arises between your mind and your heart.

For example, your mind may say, "You should never leave this job; it pays the bills," or "You should always stay in this relationship; it's better than being lonely." And your heart may counter with, "But I'm not happy here; I don't want to do this job. I'd rather be working in nature, or helping others, or doing charity work, or organizing book clubs," or "But I'm not happy in this relationship; I'd like to have more emotional connection, more friendship, and more physical intimacy with my partner."

This internal conflict is a sign that your subconscious is not happy with your Conscious Self, who's pushing the agenda of living free from repressed fears. When you start to consciously and deliberately focus more on honoring your personal values, your subconscious is naturally not going to like this because its programming is being "threatened." When your Conscious Self is more in charge of your actions, and you're about to fully integrate your Real Self into your life, your mind will start to panic. That makes sense because you haven't ventured out of your "conditioned" comfort zone before, and your subconscious doesn't know what you are going to do with this "embracing life to its fullest" business.

So get ready! Be prepared for the obstacles your subconscious will throw at you to prevent you from taking control of your life and honoring the personal values that are integral to your new, real life.

Here are three possible blockages that will come up:

1. You will procrastinate: inaction, confusion, and inertia.

2. You will face internal resistance: negative thoughts, self-doubt, and self-sabotage.

3. You will face external resistance: others questioning your actions, skeptical of your plans, and challenging your ideas.

When you leave your comfort zone, these scenarios can come at you like waves. Imagine yourself wading out into a cold ocean. Every wave (your subconscious's resistance) will try to push you back to the beach (your comfort zone). These waves are the last attempts of your subconscious to maintain control over your conditioned actions.

Therefore, it's important that you claim and acknowledge your personal values with deep conviction. If you decide the ocean is too rough and you want to go back and rest on the beach, you might lose momentum and miss the opportunity to express your Real Self in that moment. The successful Integration strategy pays off in these situations. Once you allow your Conscious Self to take charge of your actions, you can withstand the pushback of your subconscious and overcome feelings of discouragement.

5TH TRANSFORMATION TECHNIQUE: OVERCOMING OBSTACLES WITH 5 MINUTES HERE, 5 MINUTES THERE

Even with your Conscious Self in charge, it's still very difficult to sustain actions that honor your personal values and stay connected with your true essence. This difficulty is natural, as you're going against your survival animal nature, where your subconscious thrived. When you activate your higher consciousness and critical thinking skills, it's going to get easier to step outside of your comfort zone.

Once you start honoring your personal values, you get into a positive feedback loop. When you start to connect with joy and fulfillment every time you honor a personal value, you naturally want to do more of it. To get this momentum going, try to apply the 5 Minutes Here, 5 Minutes There technique.

In this strategy, you basically keep allowing yourself to experiment with your personal values and plug them into life at every opportunity, even for a few minutes. The minutes don't really count as far as your experience with personal values is concerned. The most important part of this strategy is consistency! Don't miss a day.

When honoring a personal value for five minutes a day, try to connect with how it feels internally. What are your inner feelings about this activity? Avoid justification. Stay away from explanation. Without attaching any labels, how do you feel after doing it?

If you'd like to eat healthy, do it for five minutes at breakfast, lunch, or dinner. You'd like to work out, so do it for five minutes in the morning and then again maybe right before dinner. You'd like to read more, so do it for just five minutes. Find time during your lunch break at work and read three paragraphs from your favorite book.

You see, there's no limit with the 5 Minutes Here, 5 Minutes There technique. You're now stepping out of your comfort zone, one inch a day. They'll add up soon. Before you know it, the personal values you'd like to genuinely honor become an important part of your life.

How can you use this strategy to overcome the obstacles we discussed earlier? How can this strategy help you create momentum for bringing profound and lasting change into your life? Let's review them one by one.

1. **Procrastination:** When you find yourself procrastinating, let your Conscious Self take over and apply the Doing the Opposite strategy. Usually, procrastination is the mask of your Vulnerable Self. You are dealing with a variety of repressed fears. Pushing back against what you are afraid of is necessary to break free from the stagnancy.

   In procrastination, you usually know what to do, but you avoid doing it to avoid facing your repressed fears. Now, can you take a much smaller step, without thinking about the end results or project goals? Can you experiment with what happens when you take those baby steps, with the 5 Minutes Here, 5 Minutes There technique? Pay attention to the resistance. Notice what's holding you back. Be aware of your inertia. Then take another small step and face the weight of your low self-worth and your fears of failure or not being good enough. Play the Numbers Game and activate your hidden desires of achieving success, proving that you're good, claiming your worth, with one small step at a time, with a little time here, and a little time there.

2. **Internal Resistance:** When you are fighting with negative internal talk, self-doubt, and fear, pause and observe who's behind them. Who is your Vulnerable Self or Conditioned Self that is having these negative thoughts? What are these thoughts saying about you? Can you challenge these thoughts with "What If, So What" questions and reverse engineer them to identify your repressed fears? After that, you may get curious about the original trigger events that made you feel this way. You'd be surprised, and probably shocked, to realize how much of those original feelings that turned into repressed fears are still so relevant in your current life. Today, you're basically living your past. That's why your repressed fears show up in your mind as negative thoughts. The best cure to overcome such negativity is integration. The trick is to identify the hidden desires that lie beneath the negative thoughts that come from your repressed fears. For example, if your negative thought is "I'm so lonely, no one is calling me; I have no friends." That most likely means your hidden desire is to have friends, to have an active social life. Now, integrate these two opposing forces, and then apply the Numbers Game with the 5 Minutes Here, 5 Minutes There technique to reach out to some of your friends for a small get-together.

3. **External Resistance:** When others question the conscious actions you take to honor your personal values, you may feel discouraged. You may want them to support you on this journey, yet they don't understand what you're trying to accomplish. They watch you with questioning eyes. Their attitude can be dismissive. When you feel the friction between you and others and see them as obstacles on your path, take a step back. What do you need them for? Validation? Support? Companionship? How would they know what you're going through? What kind of repressed fears are they provoking in you? Do you feel alone on your journey? Do you want to connect with them more deeply and tell them all about your journey so that you get a sense of deeper bonding and recognition from them? When they question you, question them also. What is their issue with you honoring a specific personal value? Maybe your actions of following your own path, creating your own life, trigger them and make them uncomfortable. If you'd like to remove them as obstacles and connect with them, understand where they're coming from and what their problem is with you stepping out of your comfort zone.

While you're taking these conscious steps, keep in mind that your initial goal is to strive for a healthy balance between your mind and personal values. Depending on where you are in your transformation journey, some of your ego values may still be applicable to your current life situation, and you may feel that you need to keep honoring them to continue with the trajectory of your life flow. That's okay. Just acknowledge where you are.

You may want to continue to work at your day job because your dominant ego value is predictability and recognition. But perhaps you start to allocate time, whenever you get a chance, to creativity, which is one of your personal values. You may even find new areas within your current job where you can use your creativity or honor other personal values. Keep exploring ways to bring your personal values to life.

In another scenario, let's say you are an artist. Contrary to the above example, you have creativity as one of your ego values. You feel that, through your creativity, you *should* be able to achieve fame and financial independence. But when you pressure yourself to be creative, you may find yourself frustrated, confused, and conflicted. Instead, you could choose to accept your creativity as one of your personal values and connect with joy and purpose while performing your art. You can celebrate your creativity and give yourself a chance to be famous one day—not as a goal—but as a by-product of your joyous creativity.

As you experiment with these new personal values, try to intentionally adjust and calibrate your conscious actions until you sense that you strike the right balance with your inner feelings of joy, fulfillment, and purpose. Once you create that connection, you'll realize that the obstacles start to disappear and some of your ego values and conditioned actions seem to lose their importance.

Real Life Scenario

Mark had always been a quiet, reserved man. He had followed the traditional path: a stable job, a long-term marriage, a comfortable home. Yet as he approached his mid-forties, he found himself increasingly restless and unfulfilled. Something was missing, but he couldn't quite put his finger on what it was.

His relationship with his wife had become routine, more like two roommates sharing a space than romantic partners. Their conversations were perfunctory, revolving around household chores and schedules. The spark that had once drawn them together seemed to have dimmed over the years.

This sense of disconnection extended to other areas of his life as well. Mark found himself questioning long-standing friendships, wondering what value they truly added to his life. Even his career, which he had pursued diligently for two decades, now felt hollow. He couldn't remember why he had chosen this path in the first place.

As Mark grappled with these thoughts, he realized he was at a crossroads. It was time to rediscover what truly mattered to him— his personal values that had been buried under years of conformity and expectation.

One weekend, on a whim, Mark decided to attend a hip-hop festival in the city. As he watched the crowd move to the pulsating beats, he was mesmerized. *They feel the music in their blood*, he thought to himself, both envious and inspired. Without overthinking it, he pulled out his phone and searched for "hip-hop dance classes" right there and then.

The following week, Mark found himself in a dance studio, feeling awkward but exhilarated. As he learned to relax his body and move to the rhythm, he felt a sense of freedom he hadn't experienced in years. The shy boy who never dared to dance was finally breaking free.

Energized by this new experience, Mark's curiosity led him to explore other dance forms. He stumbled upon salsa and was immediately drawn to the idea of partner dancing. Soon, he was attending Wednesday salsa nights at a local club, taking beginner classes and meeting new people.

As Mark immersed himself in this new world of dance and social interaction, he began to notice changes in other areas of his life. He felt more confident, more open to new experiences. He was forming new friendships with people who shared his newfound passion, connections that felt genuine and enriching.

This journey of self-discovery helped Mark realize what was truly important to him: expression, connection, and personal growth. He had spent years living within the confines of what he thought he should do, neglecting what he wanted to do. Now, as he moved to the rhythm of salsa or hip-hop, he was also moving to the rhythm of his own desires and values.

Mark's transformation didn't happen overnight, but with each dance class, each new friendship, each moment of joy in movement, he felt more aligned with his true nature, his Real Self. He began to see possibilities and opportunities where he once saw limitations and restrictions. His life, which had felt stagnant for so long, was now flowing with new energy and potential.

PHASE 5 REFLECTIONS

In this phase, you are trying to identify your personal values and then honor them through the actions of your Conscious Self. As you become more present through the embodiment of an objective observer, you'll sense more deeply what is happening during your experiences. In that state, you continuously connect with the impressions you feel inside. Through these conscious experiments and experiences, every little nuance, every little discovery of a personal value gets you closer to knowing parts of your Real Self.

This process of discovering personal values is like being in a dark room and looking for the light switch. You can't simply stand still and wait for the light switch to come to you. You have to start feeling around the room for furniture, walls, and other clues to help you find it. As you fumble around in the dark, you get closer to finding the purpose of your life and living according to your true essence.

For the next seven days, make a journal entry at the end of each day and write down your answers to the following questions:

1. What ego values do you honor in your current personal and professional life?

2. What did you complain about? What annoyed you? What happened today that you resented? What was missing in your life?

3. What kind of values would you like to honor tomorrow to rectify your most common complaints?

4. What are the top five personal values you discovered today?

5. Where did you apply the 5 Minutes Here, 5 Minutes There technique and how successful was it? If it wasn't successful, why did it fail? Did it create momentum?

PHASE 6

COMING OUT OF YOUR SHELL

You've finally reached the phase where you become your Real Self! You've done a lot of personal work so far. As part of this process, you have started to discover what's important to you and what kind of actions align with your true essence. At this stage, your Conscious Self makes deliberate choices to have certain experiences so you can figure out what lights up your heart, what brings you joy, what kind of values provide fulfillment. You simply ask yourself what you really like and what you don't about certain experiences. Through this playful trial and error, you get closer and closer to who you really are deep inside.

As you can appreciate, this amazing transformation of Self takes place during your everyday life. You can't sit at home and expect to discover your true essence through some mental exercises or visualizations. You have to be on the ground doing the personal work. Therefore, in a sense, bringing your personal values to life is really the Journey Within itself. This transformation is an internal process of self-discovery, rather than an adapted or borrowed principle from a concrete list of values, definitive teachings from a book, top-down directives from a teacher, or standard norms of societal doctrines.

The more you experiment with life, the more self-knowledge you acquire. And this self-knowledge and awareness is what builds the foundation your Real Self stands on. Be curious about your personal values. Try them out in real life by stepping out of your comfort zone. Tune in to how it feels internally. Then, like an old-fashioned transistor radio, consciously adjust your actions, back and forth, until you hit a frequency where you feel joy and fulfillment. Your playful and spontaneous attitude in this phase will pay off with huge rewards in the future where you eventually become your Real Self.

UNVEILING YOUR REAL SELF

Throughout this book, you have worked on bringing down the walls of your Conditioned Self, the layers of your protective mask, the forces of your hidden desires, the chains of your cultural to-dos, the obligations of societal norms, and the expectations of others. Now let me introduce you to someone who's been waiting for you at the end of the path: your Real Self.

Your Real Self is an upgrade, the more aligned, more connected version of your Conscious Self. Your Real Self is the one whose mask is removed, whose repressed fears are processed and fully integrated with its hidden desires, who lives from a place of high integrity, and whose mind, heart, and body are in complete alignment.

The Real Self is self-aware and awakened, living high above subconscious programming, and can guide your actions based on what consequences they will provoke. Your Real Self deeply understands your limiting life patterns and the root cause of your fight-or-flight defense mechanisms and automatic emotional reactions. It also sees the destructive nature of your ego values.

The Real Self lives in perfect flow and is at peace, grounded, centered in any present moment, and doesn't yield to outside distractions or the temptations of the world.

The Real Self has achieved a sense of individual freedom and emotional mastery—and has experienced glimpses of your true essence and is ready to fully embrace life with joy, fulfillment, and meaning.

Your Real Self is a solid, strong individual traveler of life, the seeker in this Journey Within, and is well connected with the inner workings of your being and intimately understands your purpose in life.

How can you bring your Real Self into your life?

LIFE OUTSIDE YOUR COMFORT ZONE

The Real Self can never be a resident of your comfort zone. Being contracted, limited, and stagnant is against the nature of your true essence. It needs to be on the go, exploring life, and learning from experiences to grow and be more conscious than yesterday when taking actions for tomorrow. Now, I suggest we put together what you've learned so far and give you a few more lampposts to light your way out of your comfort zone.

First, how do you identify that you're stuck in your comfort zone? Notice your negative patterns, conditioned behaviors, and limiting mindset that are part of your Conditioned Self and Vulnerable Self. What routines, environments, and relationships feel safe and familiar to you? Which ones don't serve you anymore and restrict your ability to live life fully? Recognizing the boundaries of your comfort zone is the first step to stepping out of it.

Second, challenge your emotional reactions that come from your repressed fears. What kind of negative thought patterns and limiting belief systems are being constantly triggered by people and situations? Examine these thoughts and beliefs behind your emotional reactions as they're the ones that hold you back from trying new things or taking risks. Ask yourself where these beliefs came from and understand them deeply by connecting them to your past.

Third, take small steps and experiment with every action you take. What's the hurry by trying to take on major life changes right away? You've been in this stagnant state for a while, and I understand the rush. But you're constructing a foundation for the rest of your life, and you want to build a strong one. Begin by trying something new and unfamiliar, even if it's small. Face the fear of the uncertainty and the unknown, and capture the opportunity for growth.

Fourth, cultivate self-awareness and self-acceptance of your polarizing forces of Conditioned Self and Vulnerable Self. What good is it to you if you start criticizing yourself and become unforgiving of your mistakes as you try to step outside your comfort zone? In a way, trying to be gentle, kind, and patient with yourself is a way of going against your self-critical Vulnerable Self. Notice when you're feeling some kind of resistance or anxiety and celebrate your courage instead of your success.

Fifth, the real life is outside of your comfort zone, and the only way to experience such a colorful, fruitful, and rich life is to seek out new experiences and perspectives. How would it look if you intentionally exposed yourself to different people, places, and activities that challenge your worldview? What if you traveled to new destinations, engaged with diverse communities, or tried hobbies you've never explored before? Would that break the monotony, the stagnancy that you've felt stuck and trapped in for so many years?

The journey of stepping outside your comfort zone is not about perfection or radical transformation overnight, it's a brick in your foundation that you're building for your new life, the real life, your Real Self gets to guide you through. Such high flow energy is all about gradually expanding your horizons, building resilience, and discovering your personal freedom and fulfillment that can come from embracing the unknown. With patience, courage, and a willingness to learn, you can unlock a new level of personal growth and write your own story.

6TH TRANSFORMATION STRATEGY: BLAZING YOUR OWN TRAIL

When you start expressing your Real Self, you don't have to copy anybody else, follow their advice, imitate what they're doing, or follow their game plans. Can you simply stay on your path, in your own lane? Can you follow your inclinations, inner feelings, and self-awareness toward your personal values and find ways to honor them?

If you can stay completely independent of others' influences and remain unaffected by their opinions and values that they impose upon you, life will open doors to you with unexpected opportunities. As these opportunities arise, can you use them to leave your comfort zone? Can you accept these invitations that life presents to you and make a conscious effort to honor yet another personal value by trying something new?

When you take these conscious steps, they won't go to waste. Every step becomes forward motion, creating deeper alignments with your true essence. That's where you start to blaze your own trail. You're unstoppable. The more you get out there with conscious actions to experiment with your personal values, the clearer your path to self-realization becomes. Consider these efforts as claiming your own life, mastering your own domain. You are here to create your own value system, adopt your own homegrown principles, express your own voice, and stamp your own signature onto your life.

Such an act is not selfish, as long as your value-based framework doesn't encroach on others' boundaries. Blazing your own trail means you don't need to bother others with your opinions. You pay attention to your own life, to your own shortcomings. Mastering your domain means cleaning your own house first. If you want a clean neighborhood, start with your own front porch. That's how you blaze your own trail and, hopefully, inspire others to join you on the Journey Within.

6TH TRANSFORMATION TECHNIQUE: EXPRESSING YOUR REAL SELF WITH HEART

The purpose of becoming your Real Self is to live your life according to the principles of your true essence so that you can find joy and fulfillment in your life. You can only experience the purpose of your life through the expression of your Real Self. This phase is pivotal because it may very well introduce you to your life's work. As you start expressing your essence, you will slowly come to realize the unique thoughts, visions, talent, creativity, and skill set that you naturally and innately possess. You just need to take action to apply them more consciously to your life. You will experience several feelings along the way that reassure you that you're on the right path.

Joy and Inspiration

Joy and inspiration can only be described as inner feelings of high flow. This connection with a deeper creativity may be a new phenomenon for you. Looking back, you may feel that you have lived a sheltered life with a focus on things that didn't bring much joy. As you feel more connected with your Real Self and show interest in exploring new areas of creativity, you start to feel the expansion of your energy. When you feel this high energy, you see new possibilities that can lead you to new potentials in your future. You deeply feel joy that invites you to be more curious about what you can create, which in turn inspires you to fully experience life through your own self-expression.

Such joy and inspiration offsets guilt and self-judgment. When you connect more intimately with your Real Self, you naturally feel self-acceptance and self-respect, and gain access to a deeper creativity that flows through you and out of you. Together, these drive you to embrace life to its fullest, which puts you in alignment with your true nature and essence.

Gratitude

Gratitude is the act of recognizing and appreciating the positive aspects of life, including the kindness of others, the beauty of nature, or even small everyday moments and comforts that bring you close to your Real Self. Such acknowledgment brings a completely different perspective to your life—one which celebrates life and who you really are as you march the path toward self-realization.

Therefore, practicing gratitude can have a profound impact on your personal growth and transformation journey from living in your comfort zone (very little to be grateful for) to embracing more well-being and fullness of life (plenty of things to be grateful for). Let's review a few commonly known steps to incorporate gratitude into your life and see which ones resonate with you and stick as your daily routine in your new life:

1. **Keep a Gratitude Journal:** Write down a few things you are thankful for each day. This practice can help you focus on the positives and can boost your mood and overall outlook, especially when you're trying to go against your Vulnerable Self, who seems to be always in that victim state.

2. **Express Gratitude to Others:** Regularly tell people around you why you appreciate them. This can strengthen your relationships and increase your feelings of connection and support, especially when you get to know yourself, these interactions provide more meaningful exchanges for you and others.

3. **Focus on Growth from Challenges:** Reflect on difficult experiences and identify lessons learned or strengths gained, cultivating an attitude of gratitude

even for challenges, when you consciously take actions to neutralize your Conditioned Self and Vulnerable Self, and create an integrated life.

Incorporating these practices into your life can lead to a sense of groundedness, resiliency, and determination to become your Real Self. Over time, gratitude can become a natural tool to override your conditioned behavior, continuously helping you grow on your personal transformation journey.

Forgiveness

Forgiveness is releasing others from the responsibility to act according to your expectations, beliefs, or value system. Usually, you feel the need to forgive when someone has hurt you, betrayed you, disrespectfully crossed your boundaries, and so on. From that point of view, forgiveness is the healthy process of a victim taking their power back, but it's still very hard to let go of the past.

However, when you process your emotional wounds and become your Real Self with high integrity levels, opportunities for forgiveness and reconciliation of past hurts naturally appear in front of you for resolution. As a result, forgiveness acknowledges your pain but accepts the wrongdoing of others, moving you into a state of reconciliation and openness. This acceptance is the opposite of judgment, and it's where parties come together for mutual understanding and connection.

These inner feelings of forgiveness are not available until your Real Self feels that inner strength of a full integration between the mind, heart, and body. By understanding your own nature and conditioning, you will be able to help the other person understand how and why they hurt you and eventually forgive them.

Compassion

Compassion naturally arises within you when you truly understand your Conditioned Self and get to know your Real Self; otherwise, how can you feel what others are going through? In this state, you will naturally feel compassion for others and a deep understanding of their repressed fears and hidden desires and why they do things the way they do. This inner knowledge and connection with others opens the way for you to spread love and compassion throughout your community.

Compassion is the opposite of hate, anger, resentment, and rage. When you gain this deeper understanding of others and their suffering, you will begin to drop your labels, judgments, and perceptions. But without first knowing your Conditioned Self, it's difficult to know and understand somebody else's.

Try not to force compassion as a mental construct with thoughts like, *I should be more compassionate now,* when you're about to emotionally react to someone. As you expand your self-awareness and knowledge of your Conditioned Self, compassion will naturally be part of your inner feelings of high integrity.

Feeling deep connection with your true essence is rejuvenating. It injects a powerful energy into your actions. When you are filled with enthusiasm and have a new outlook on life, you want to get up in the morning and start your day as soon as you can. This excitement pushes you into an exhilarating creative process.

You may find yourself connecting with old inspirations and dreams that you once had. New visions, ideas, and aspirations will push you further into new areas of interest. You may start nurturing your old interests and incorporate them into your life. Follow your creativity. This is the birth of your Real Self and your life's work. Claim your uniqueness and keep walking toward self-realization, your highest potential, joyfully.

Real Life Scenario

Travis had always felt there was more to life than what he'd been living. For years, he'd pushed down his true feelings and desires, conforming to what he thought others expected of him. But lately, maybe as a result of taking conscious actions against his Conditioned Self, a restlessness had been growing inside him, a yearning to break free and show the world his authentic Self.

One crisp morning, Travis decided to take a walk on the beach to honor one of his personal values of being in nature. As he strolled along the shore, he found himself noticing things he'd never paid attention to before: the intricate patterns left by receding waves, the way sunlight danced on ocean waves, the symphony of colors in a single shell. It was as if he was seeing the world through a new set of eyes.

Inspired by this newfound awareness, Travis began spending more time at the beach, immersing himself in nature. His beach walks became a daily ritual, a time for reflection and connection with his inner Self, with his true nature. He started to feel more grounded, more in tune with his heart's true values.

As Travis spent more time outdoors, he felt a creative spark ignite within him. Words began to flow, and he found himself writing poetry for the first time in his life. His verses captured the beauty he saw in nature, the emotions stirred by a sunset, the peace found in watching flocks of pelicans fly by.

But words weren't enough to fully express what Travis was experiencing. He picked up a camera, eager to capture the visual poetry he encountered every day. He began rising before dawn, chasing the first rays of sunlight as they painted the world in gold. His lens found beauty in unexpected places as he strolled on the streets of the city. The play of light on city buildings intrigued him. The changing colors of leaves on boardwalks fascinated him.

As Travis delved deeper into his creative pursuits, he discovered a passion for poetic narrative writing. He wanted to describe not just what he saw but what he felt and sensed during his intimate encounters with nature and city. His writing became a blend of vivid imagery and heartfelt emotion, capturing moments of connection and wonder.

With each passing day, Travis felt more alive, more authentic and more real. He was no longer hiding parts of himself or trying to fit into a mold. Instead, he was allowing his true nature to shine through in every photograph, every poem, every piece of writing.

The urge to share his creations grew stronger. Travis started a blog, pouring his heart into articles that showcased his photography and writing. It felt like a coming-out party for his Real Self. He couldn't wait to share his newfound passion with friends and family, to show them the world as he now saw it.

As Travis's website expanded with his writings and images, so did his confidence. He was no longer afraid to show up as his Real Self. He followed his intuition, trusting his gut feelings and the values that resonated in his heart, in his soul. His creativity flowed freely, uninhibited by fear or self-doubt.

Through this journey of self-expression, Travis discovered that being true to himself wasn't just personally fulfilling—it also allowed him to connect more deeply with others. His authentic self-expression and the way his Real Self showed up in the world inspired those around him, encouraging them to embrace their own unique perspectives and creative impulses. One day, he sat on the couch, looking outside the window, hearing the drops of the fall rain, and thought to himself how content and fulfilled he felt inside.

PHASE 6 REFLECTIONS

Now that we are in this phase, the rubber really hits the road. When addressing the questions below at the end of each day, I hope you get a sense that your Real Self has touched the ground. Yes, your Real Self is in the house, embodied within your actions, and is ready to represent your true essence. With each step and every action, you enter into the world and claim your place.

That doesn't mean you're getting fame, success, or wealth. It only means that you are being you, your real you. The rest is just noise. Once you feel that you have become your Real Self, the one you were born to be, the enjoyment of your inner feelings is much sweeter than any outside gratification. Even so, as others recognize that you are living from a place of authenticity, you may receive plenty of gratification, which only becomes the cherry on top of the joy and fulfillment you already feel.

For the next seven days, make a journal entry at the end of each day and write down your answers to the following questions:

1. How did you use the Blazing Your Own Trail strategy when honoring your top personal values and integrating them into your life?

2. How did you experience your Conscious Self and what kind of conscious actions did you take to get a glimpse of your Real Self?

3. What kind of obstacles did you encounter when trying to honor your personal values and what actions did you take to overcome them?

4. What people, places, or scenarios have you identified as your comfort zone, and how did you consciously try to step out of that comfort zone?

5. What inner feelings did you experience when you expressed your Real Self with personal values in a high integrity state?

PHASE 7

LIVING WITH PURPOSE

You finally made it! In the last six phases, through the study of your own life experiences, you have realized that whatever you experience today in your life is exactly what your subconscious programming wants you to experience. You now understand that your life is completely structured to avoid your repressed fears and perpetuate your hidden desires so you never face your vulnerability and insecurities. By going against your conditioned actions, and eventually integrating your opposing masks, you have allowed your Conscious Self to discover your personal values and slowly make space to become your Real Self and start living with more joy and fulfillment.

The final phase is all about finding the purpose or the calling you've been looking for. If you have already connected with the key exercises in each phase, you may already feel that your life is shifting, subtly and profoundly, and opening more doors for you to bring more purpose into your life.

You have probably already noticed that the journey is not linear. That's why it's a lifelong process. There will be ups and downs throughout. No matter where you are in your journey, always remember that roadblocks are only there for you to learn more about your Vulnerable Self and Conditioned Self and to give your Real Self a chance to emerge stronger. Never forget that you can always connect with your Conscious Self to bring more joy and fulfillment into your life. Just keep walking on your beautiful Journey Within.

From here on out, the only action you need to take is to open your arms and heart to receive the opportunities your Real Self has started attracting to your life. Simply walk through each door that is aligned with your personal values to express your Real Self. Joyfully share your true essence and uniqueness with the world and people around you.

GOING WITH THE FLOW OF LIFE

What you're about to do is not an easy task. Such an assignment requires a deep level of integration of your Conditioned Self and Vulnerable Self to help you connect with your inner power to let go of your attachments to outcomes and safety and instead embrace the natural flow of life.

To that extent, how well can you recognize when you're caught up in chasing ego-driven goals and values that don't truly fulfill you? How well can you let go of the need for control, certainty, and rigid plans for your life? How much can you trust the unfolding process of becoming your Real Self and be open to new opportunities that arise organically?

When you worked on discovering your personal values, you identified them so that you can connect with what truly matters to you, such as your inherent desires, passions, and purpose. These personal values eventually become your inner guidance to stay in the flow for joy and fulfillment, instead of chasing success from outside resources for fleeting moments of happiness.

Be aware that such personal values are always subject to change. As you grow and expand your self-awareness, and step into the unknown and uncertainty with courage, you may adapt new values. Acceptance of such evolution of your Real Self can be an indestructible power behind your Journey Within and personal transformation.

Therefore, deeply connect with the personal values you can't live without. Set your sights on what's important to you and keep taking advantage of the opportunities that show up for you to fulfill that personal value. When you connect with the joy and fulfillment that arises within you, there's no turning back to where you were before. Without getting caught by the lure of the destination, focus on appreciating the beauty of the path as you step into new beginnings.

When you embody these principles, you can begin to unlock a sense of personal freedom, immense joy, content fulfillment, and wonderous magic that arises naturally when you fully surrender control and courageously live in alignment with your personal values and your Real Self.

7TH TRANSFORMATION STRATEGY: SURRENDERING WITH EFFORTLESS ACTION

When you only focus on your life experiences and nothing else, you reach a flow state where your actions feel effortless yet result from tremendous integration of your mind, heart, and body. You may feel a little strange when you get to this high flow state, as it's difficult to fathom how you can be active and surrender at the same time.

Active normally implies some kind of activity, movement, or motion. Surrendering often indicates passivity. However, in this context, it means suspension of fears and desires. You're really not giving up anything, not your boundaries, not your self-respect. You're not a pushover by any means. However, you take action when necessary, and only when you're called to.

Surrendering with Effortless Action is not about giving in or being passive, but about patiently waiting for alignment in situations that warrant action toward your personal values and expression of your true essence. Such deep connection with life and what's happening in any given moment is very difficult to sustain for long periods of time as it requires you to be fully present to see the new opportunities as invitations for your next action.

Surrendering also presents an interesting twofold consideration when making life decisions. The first consideration is to practice going with the flow and seeing where the current alignment or misalignment (i.e., the existence of a conflict) leads you. The other consideration is to notice any resistance to taking certain actions that claim your personal values. One of life's biggest dilemmas is the duality that your subconscious programming creates in your head. It's that internal conflict of repressed fears and hidden desires that leads to the illusionary mental construct of duality—good versus bad, right versus wrong, success versus failure, beautiful versus ugly, rich versus poor, bad breakup versus great relationship, and so on.

When we're at a lower awareness level, these two opposite and extreme possibilities seem to be the only options available for us to consider. This black-and-white approach to life comes from our fight-or-flight defense mechanisms that actually disserve us because it creates a sense of contraction, confusion, heaviness, and suffering that affects the quality of your life and makes taking effortless actions difficult to execute.

But as you integrate your repressed fears and hidden desires and, hence, are able to break free from your comfort zone, you enter that high flow state, and this polarized outlook on life starts to fizzle away. Your internal conflicts, indecisiveness, and lack of clarity in your life decisions turn into ease in decision-making, into clear vision on consequences of your particular actions, and into internal peace that stems from your ever-growing confidence.

When you are fully present and tuned in to how to proceed with an opportunity as your Real Self, you're basically responding to what a situation requires instead of initiating action on your own. This kind of response, the Effortless Action, requires no thinking, strategizing, or constructing a specific goal, as each decision stems from your inner knowing, from your inner alignment, which literally guides you closer and closer toward self-realization without any mental construct of how it should look or be.

When you sense this presence and take Effortless Action as you fully surrender to a situation, you experience the highest possible number of synchronicities in your life. The invitation of life through these experiences is for you to understand that you have a certain inner power, a sixth sense, a deep level of intuition that promotes higher alignment between your mind, heart, and body.

During these experiences of your Real Self, you will catch yourself in this high flow state where Effortless Action is part of your daily life. You'll realize at this level that a trigger flies by without affecting you emotionally, as your Conditioned Self is no longer carrying a heavy mask. You'll recognize that you are no longer getting pulled into your old ways of defending your vulnerabilities and insecurities, nor getting stuck in your old destructive habits. Instead, you get a sense of an energetic shift, a consciousness shift, where Effortless Action is more available and more possible to do.

When you respond to the stream of life coming to you, you basically deal with whatever is in front of you in that very moment. You just wait to act until the right time, not a second too soon, not a second too late. And when you move, you choose your actions according to your own personal values, all aligned with the mental, emotional, and physical layers of your Real Self, instead of the values that others impose on you or expect you to live by.

STARTING A NEW LIFE

I hope you have finally met your Real Self. Now you know how to utilize the opportunities life offers to bring aspects of your uniqueness to the surface. Throughout your Journey Within, you have experienced that the higher your awareness level, the better your life flow. All you need to do is take actions that teach you more about yourself and raise your consciousness level. To test whether you are taking the right steps, check in with yourself about whether you feel joy and a sense of fulfillment. Life will take care of the rest and guide you toward self-realization.

Imagine a musician trying to get perfect pitch by adjusting their instrument—they tighten and loosen the strings until they feel satisfied by the sound. Your journey toward becoming your Real Self is much like this tuning process. When you reach your perfect pitch, meaning that you can maintain the connection to your true essence for longer periods of time, you will be able to express your unique Real Self as it naturally manifests in every aspect of your life. In a sense, these manifestations are the beginning of a major life transformation.

How do you keep your connection to higher levels of consciousness? You must consistently work on expressing your Real Self. New beginnings represent the ever-increasing moments of feeling joy and expressing your Real Self. It's not one single door that you need to go through to step into a new beginning. It's many—a gradual path that you proceed down in different aspects of your life. *It's not merely a change in habits but a change in the way you see, how you respond, and how you experience life.*

ACKNOWLEDGING SYNCHRONICITIES

You are probably feeling it already. When you step into new beginnings, you are filled with joy and hope. It feels like you are starting your life anew. You have the enthusiasm and motivation of someone who is about to graduate from high school or college with hopes, aspirations, and dreams for the future. Take a moment to notice any new possibilities that have already started showing up as you experience the glimpses of a magical and harmonious flow of life.

This incredible alignment of seemingly unrelated events that coincide in improbable ways are called synchronicities. These events may or may not have significant messages for you, yet they guide you toward deeper revelations, insightful reflections, and personally beneficial outcomes that lead you to meaningful experiences. When you become more and more your Real Self, the frequency of these occurrences increases.

During those synchronized moments, you feel connected with your true essence and experience this almost sacred alignment with the people you interact with and situations you encounter. All you have to do is joyfully observe and enjoy these random things coming together and opening doors to more experiences where your Real Self steps on the stage of life, guided by this magical flow. Acknowledge these invitations and, without thinking too much, simply walk through with your heart. Synchronicities are full of fun and bring so much joy.

Here are some examples of the synchronicities I have experienced:

- Finding convenient parking spots during the busiest time of day
- Looking at the clock or my phone randomly throughout the day and consistently seeing the same repeating numbers, like 11:11, 2:22, or 3:33

- Wondering about someone I haven't heard from in a while or thinking of connecting with someone, and then receiving a call from them out of the blue
- Getting into my car and hearing the same song on the radio repeatedly, whose lyrics carry a special message for a challenging situation I'm facing
- Running into an old friend who introduces me to someone who teaches the kind of martial art I have wanted to practice for a while
- Finding a book on the table at a coffee shop that I intended to buy a long time ago
- Randomly discovering that the course I always wanted to take is about to start the following week
- Somehow finding tickets to a sold-out lecture of someone whom I have been following for years
- Meeting someone who connects me to someone else who agrees to rent me their office for my coaching practice on an hourly basis, which is located fifteen minutes from where I work
- Running late to a sold-out play, where the usher seats me in one of two vacant spots in the sixth row at the orchestra level, only to find out at intermission that my ticket has the same row and seat number, but for the second balcony

When you experience synchronicities such as these, pause and observe their magic and smile. Life goes beyond what we see with our naked eyes. What kind of synchronicities do you experience these days? How do you feel about them?

7TH TRANSFORMATION TECHNIQUE: FOCUSING ON THE EXPERIENCE

Synchronicities may be signs that you are on the right path. Do you remember what the flow of life was like before you started your journey? Wasn't it like a rollercoaster, with frequent ups and downs of emotions, and moments of happiness followed by moments of despair? Didn't you feel good about your job one day, and then the next, something would happen with your boss and you found yourself looking for your next gig? Didn't you feel like your partner was the best thing that ever happened to you at certain times, and then other times you questioned your relationship?

After traveling on this journey for a while, you are starting to sense that the flow of your life is turning into a comfortable river ride. Frequent and abrupt ups and downs have disappeared from your life. Through synchronicities and opportunities that are aligned with your true essence, a smoother flow has appeared in your life, allowing you to express your Real Self more and more and connect with the joy of life.

At times, though it's very rare now, you may lose your way and end up back on that emotional rollercoaster. You may be confused about how many opportunities are in front of you, and your subconscious programming kicks in again. You may not know which opportunity to choose or what door to go through. Your decisions may be influenced by hidden desires that are still active. In these moments, try to tune in to your personal values. After making a few mistakes that lead you back to your limiting life patterns, you'll intuitively sense which opportunities are aligned with your true essence, with your Real Self, and which ones are not.

Therefore, your focus should be only on your experiences. By learning from the negative outcomes, you become more discerning about your actions in the future and align them better next time with what's important to you.

If you run into situations where you keep experiencing outcomes that you don't like, investigate the circumstances and your motives at a deeper level to figure out if your Conditioned Self's hidden desires are in charge of your decisions. When you realize why your actions are not fully aligned with your true essence, treat it as a learning experience. Try to reconnect with your personal values, no matter how many times you trap yourself by jumping into opportunities with hidden desires.

When you realize where your actions are coming from and focus on your experience, you will easily realize that you have chosen a door that doesn't lead you down the path you thought it would. Then you can use your learning from previous experience and simply close that door. If you are meant to go another direction, life will open a new door pretty quickly. At the end of the day, every life experience expands your self-awareness and deepens your understanding, even though you may not recognize its lessons or benefits at the time.

APPLYING THE GOLDEN RULE

No matter how you decide to honor your personal values in your life, apply the Golden Rule: treat others the way you want to be treated and also treat yourself with the same respect, acceptance, and compassion that you show to others. The Golden Rule sets a high standard for your conscious actions that will carry the energy of high integrity.

Be aware that you tend to cross the line of the Golden Rule when you proceed with an individualistic, self-centered action because you feel vulnerable and insecure. You may naturally feel threatened when you're trying to expand your boundaries with your new personal values and others resist or object to your intentions. In these cases, keep working on fine-tuning your actions toward your personal values and self-realization and use these trigger events, obstacles, and objections as opportunities to get to know your Conditioned Self. Try to get out of your automatic fight-or-flight defense mode and connect with your inner power to allow your Conscious Self to reemerge with curiosity, awareness, and understanding. Only then, reconnect with joy, gratitude, forgiveness, and compassion to connect with your Real Self and with others. A new life with deeper purpose is about to emerge.

REAL LIFE SCENARIO

Liz had always been a successful marketing executive, climbing the corporate ladder with determination and skill. But lately, she'd been feeling a nagging sense of emptiness, as if something vital was missing from her life. It wasn't until she stumbled upon a documentary about global poverty that she felt a spark ignite within her.

As days turned into weeks, Liz found herself increasingly drawn to the plight of impoverished communities in Africa and Asia. Her evenings, once filled with mindless TV shows and scrolling through social media, were now consumed by research and reading. She barely noticed the transition, but her life was slowly being reshaped by a newfound sense of purpose.

Books on world history, economic inequality, and international development began piling up on her nightstand. Liz's hunger for knowledge was insatiable. She delved deep into the root causes of global poverty, exploring how historical events and international policies had contributed to the current state of affairs in many African and Asian nations.

As her understanding grew, so did her passion to make a difference. Liz realized that her day job, while successful, no longer fulfilled her in the same way. The excitement she felt when researching solutions to poverty far outweighed any satisfaction she derived from her marketing campaigns.

This new compass in her life transformed her everyday experiences. Mundane tasks took on new meaning as she saw them as steps toward her greater goal. Even her conversations changed, becoming more purposeful and focused on global issues and potential solutions.

Driven by her growing passion, Liz took a bold step and formed a nonprofit organization. It started small, but her marketing skills and genuine enthusiasm helped it grow quickly. She found herself surrounded by like-minded individuals who shared her vision for a more equitable world.

As her nonprofit gained traction, Liz felt an increasing pull away from her corporate job. The contrast between her day-to-day work and her true calling became starker with each passing day. After much soul-searching and careful planning, she made the courageous decision to leave her executive position and dedicate herself fully to her nonprofit work.

This wasn't just a career change for Liz; it was a complete life transformation. She had aligned her daily activities with her deepest personal values, and the result was a life filled with purpose and meaning. The challenges were plenty, but Liz approached each one with enthusiasm, seeing them as opportunities to grow and make a real impact.

As Liz embarked on this new chapter, she felt a sense of adventure and fulfillment she had never experienced before. Her life had become a mission—a journey dedicated to finding innovative solutions to poverty and resource inequality around the world. And while the road ahead was long and complex, Liz knew she was exactly where she needed to be, living a life true to her values and making a difference in the world as her Real Self.

PHASE 7 REFLECTIONS

This is the grand finale! Now you know what the seven phases of personal transformation are all about. You have the map in your hands to embark on your Journey Within any time you feel disconnected from life. Every day, watch for your complaints. Whether you're at home, at work, with friends, or with family, tune in to your inner feelings and note what is missing from your life.

For the next seven days, make a journal entry at the end of each day and write down your answers to the following questions:

1. What does stepping into new beginnings mean to you, and how do the new opportunities show up in your life?

2. What kind of synchronicities have you started experiencing?

3. How hard is it to focus on your experiences and learn about your Real Self, versus losing your awake state and emotionally reacting?

4. How many times have you thought about the Golden Rule and consciously adjusted your actions?

5. What is the purpose of your life, and how strongly do you feel it in your daily actions on your path to self-realization?

CONCLUSION

Building Trust and Flow

If you asked me what I've gained from my personal transformation journey over the last eighteen years, I'd tell you that it's the unyielding trust in life that I feel deep inside today. When I can hold onto this trust, I feel invincible and deeply connected to my inner power, which helps me break down the walls of safety and security again and again. After all, shattering my comfort zone ultimately led me build a new life that is beyond my dreams and exists far away from the borders of the matrix I used to live in, where my body was sick and my life contracted.

After that call in July 2006 with Naz, the intuitive healer, I felt the invitation to dedicate my entire life to get to know myself and share my findings with others. I was innately curious about human conditioning and how it affects our lives. By experiencing every situation with deep introspection, I was lucky to actively gather enough self-knowledge to understand who I was at my core.

Such valuable information ultimately led me to truly experience life to its fullest and helped me gain insights about my personal values. When I discovered them, one by one, I then realized what was important to me. This deep connection with my Real Self helped me leave the matrix and start living according to my own spiritual principles with self-respect, high integrity, and deep personal honor.

Back then, I didn't have any plans to leave the corporate world or my marriage. I was enjoying my newfound curiosity about my life and my Real Self. However, the moment I started connecting with my true essence, unexpected situations started to arise, as if they were waiting for me to open my eyes to a new reality. Suddenly, I found myself in the middle of my awakening with an amazing flow!

Life simply started to open its doors to me. These doors were hidden before and could have remained invisible had I not taken the steps to break the barriers of the matrix. I can't imagine where I would have ended up had I not decided to follow the breadcrumbs life was carefully putting in front of me. I was in such a high flow state that I never felt I needed to plan anything. Everything, whatever I needed at the time, unfolded in front of me. That's how I was able to build a deep trust in life that has never faded away.

One day, that high flow state randomly led me to run into my college friend from Istanbul on the streets of San Francisco after fifteen years of not being in touch. I don't know how to explain to you in simple words how serendipitous this encounter was; it eventually changed my life. My friend's name was Nil, and she was the one who introduced me to Reiki healing and to my Qigong teacher, Master Zhou. Both modalities helped me overcome the exhausting cycle of my sinus infections. Immediately thereafter, I decided to take various courses to pursue the Reiki energy healing path and learn Qigong meditation practices.

Of course, the more these modalities helped me heal, the more enthusiastic I became to share my explorations with my colleagues at work. The word got out, and everybody started inviting me to have coffee or lunch meetings with them, hoping to get help on various life decisions they were dealing with. During these interactions, I was able to share some of the techniques I learned, which helped them have clarity and better judgment on their own personal situations.

One meeting after another, the accounts payable specialist on my team, Christina, thought I could be a good life coach. I immediately refused her suggestion. After all, I was a VP of finance, and we had some accounting to do. Against my will, she secretly created a Yelp page on my behalf and left my first five-star review. Approximately a month later, someone called me and asked me for a Reiki session. I was thrilled, as well as extremely nervous, as my first client happened to be a very experienced therapist looking for a Reiki session.

She became my first regular weekly client. Our sessions went very well. I learned a lot from her, which made me more confident about what I could offer. Soon after, I had three more clients join my weekly schedule. I would joyfully schedule them during my lunch times, or meet them early in the morning before work, or late at night on my way home.

Slowly, the numbers that I had to deal with in the finance and accounting department didn't mean much to me compared to what I was experiencing outside of work. It was clear to me that my personal values had dramatically changed. It was inevitable that I had to leave the corporate world. I could feel it, and there was no internal resistance to such a possibility. Around that time, my boss realized that my heart was no longer in my work. He and the head of HR pulled me aside one day and told me that I was fired.

At the time, due to recession, and due to some bad personal decisions, my wife and I were almost bankrupt. We owed tens of thousands of dollars to contractors and our money was tied in dead investments. We moved out of our big house and started living in a studio apartment in Palo Alto. At the time, my wife was the only one earning income as a contractor at below market hourly rate. Looking at my calendar, I could see only four clients who had sessions on a weekly basis—which meant about a 90 percent reduction to my income level.

Times were tough; understandably my wife gently suggested that I look for additional income and take up some temporary accounting jobs to help with the finances. However, I couldn't fulfill her suggestion. Somehow, I felt strongly that things were going to work out for us. I knew that I just needed to keep taking steps on this path to become my Real Self and answer my calling. I asked her to give me six months. Within three to four months, I was getting more calls, and my client base doubled. Within a year, I had close to fifteen clients a week and was holding a weekly workshop with a few people in attendance.

I don't know how it all happened. It was as if an invisible hand was orchestrating everything, and all I had to do was enter the doors life presented in front of me. Of course, I've lost that magic touch many times since then. Whenever I planned, strategized, thought about my next steps, I always fell out of grace, lost trust, and got diverted from that high flow. However, the moment I consciously came back to the 7 Phases of Transformation and followed the steps that I shared with you here, I always hopped back on the path to self-realization with even deeper trust.

When you truly embrace each opportunity that lies in front of you, you naturally connect with your Real Self. The opposite is also true: when you open your arms to embody your true nature, life grants what you wish for. New doors appear in front of you almost out of the blue. Then you get to choose which one appeals to you the most and go through it with enthusiasm and excitement. Suddenly, you find yourself in a high flow state. When you strike that energy and connect with your Real Self, all sorts of unexpected, positive situations start to arise in your life.

It's not out of the ordinary that people in that high flow state become more productive and efficient at their job and get unexpected promotions. Some of them stumble upon new careers that eventually become their "calling." Many deepen their connection and rekindle their intimacy with their partner. Some report that their relationships with their kids have never been better. Some get artsy, some get creative, some find their soulmate, some go on cruises, while others lose themselves in nature hikes, or mountain tops, or in mesmerizing tunes of jazz bands, or resonating sounds of classical music in city halls.

It's completely up to you how much of your Real Self you'd like to present to the world. Maybe you begin to study new subjects that nurture your true nature. Maybe you follow a healthier lifestyle by consciously choosing your food and being more active and engaged with your own nourishment. Maybe you start to appreciate life as it is and are grateful for what you already have. Whatever path you choose, you're bound to feel a sense of fulfillment and a deeper meaning that stems from knowing who you really are and realizing what the purpose of your life is.

These beautiful experiences and magical moments of new opportunities are only a glimpse of what lies ahead for you. Enjoy these experiences, and at the same time, remember that the Journey Within toward self-realization is a lifelong process. From time to time, you may notice that your Conditioned Self reappears in your life. It's inevitable. You will run into yet another limiting life pattern, finding yourself intensely reacting to a trigger event emotionally. Boom, all of a sudden you have taken two steps back.

This back and forth is normal and is part of the personal growth and transformation process. Any time you feel you have tightened your boundaries and fallen into your subconscious conditioned state again, use this withdrawal as an opportunity to re-recognize the mask your Conditioned Self wears and the vulnerabilities and insecurities of your Vulnerable Self that your subconscious harbors.

When you regroup and recenter your energy, life will start to bring new opportunities again. These synchronicities are gateways. Explore whatever resonates with your heart. Instead of trying to *become* this or that, *honor* your personal values that make you feel complete, joyful, and fulfilled. You don't have to make plans or set grand goals beyond your very next step. Just walk through what's in front of you.

Such steps, hesitant at first, assured later, will only build more trust in your Real Self and in the universe that life is on your side when you're living with integrity and presence. The rewards of surrendering to such flow without control but with full trust and inner knowing lead to experiences of profound ease, joy, and purpose as you let go the past and embrace the organic yet high flow of your new and real life. Simply step back and witness your life expanding in unanticipated, meaningful ways and allow yourself to develop deep, compassionate connections with others who are on a similar path to self-realization.

As joy, fulfillment, and purpose become your guides, you slowly take your unique place in the mosaic of humanity. When you honor the requirements and responsibilities of such a role, your calling naturally turns into a valuable service to others, where you get the chance to express your newly discovered innate gifts. Ultimately, the path to self-realization invites you to lift yourself up from the confines of the matrix to help others awaken to their Real Selves.

After all, everything and everyone is interconnected, and the collective consciousness embodies all aspects of you, as you're all aspects of humanity.

A Personal Invitation to Further Your Journey

Dear Reader,

As you close this book, your journey of self-discovery and growth doesn't have to end here. I'd like to invite you to take the next step alongside other like-minded individuals who are passionate about personal development.

Join me for an enriching experience:
"The Journey Within"
A Free 7-Week Workshop

This transformative program is designed to deepen the insights you've gained in this book and provide you with practical tools for ongoing personal growth.

To secure your spot and continue your journey, please visit:
www.R2R.org/Journey-Within

I look forward to connecting with you
and walking on this meaningful journey together.

ABOUT THE AUTHOR

Arda Ozdemir is a spiritual mentor and relationship coach who left the corporate world to pursue his calling to help people rise above their ordinary life and achieve their highest potential through realizing their true nature, their Real Self that leads them to joy, fulfillment, and purpose.

Arda has empowered thousands of clients in the last fifteen years to break free from their limiting conditioned subconscious programming and experience profound transformation and self-realization by going through the 7 Phases of Transformation.

In addition to his individual and couples sessions, Arda has founded the Rise 2 Realize Institute to offer his teachings free of charge through various group classes, workshops, and retreats, including a five-week Journey Within workshop offered once a year. You can view the upcoming free events at www.R2R.org/events.

Arda is the host of the Rise 2 Realize Podcast and has previously published three books, *Emotional Mastery for Relationships* (2025), *The Art of Becoming Unstuck* (2021), and *The Seeker's Manual* (2014).

Arda's ultimate mission is to raise consciousness and awareness in the collective to cultivate peace, harmony, and unity in the world.

www.ingramcontent.com/pod-product-compliance
Lightning Source LLC
Chambersburg PA
CBHW060451080526
44584CB00015B/1408